THE TIMES

working in
ENGLISH
LANGUAGE
teaching

FRANCESCA
TARGET

**KOGAN
PAGE**

I am extremely grateful to my friends, colleagues and ex-students who agreed to be interviewed for this book. People were unfailingly helpful and generous with their time and very willing to share their experience of ELT.

First published in 2002

Kogan Page Limited
120 Pentonville Road
London N1 9JN

British Library Cataloguing in Publication Data

A CIP record for this book is available from the British Library.

ISBN 0 7494 3585 2

Typeset by JS Typesetting, Wellingborough, Northants
Printed and bound in Great Britain by Bell & Bain Ltd, Glasgow

MA COURSES IN LANGUAGE TEACHING AND TESTING AT THE UNIVERSITY OF READING

The University of Reading offers a range of master's level courses for language teaching professionals, including the MA in TEFL, the MA in Applied Linguistics, and the MA in Language Testing. The students are a mix of native and non-native teachers who work in schools, colleges and universities in their own countries or elsewhere around the world.

Typically the students have a few years of teaching experience (although they can be accepted with just one year's full time teaching experience). They come to do a master's course for several reasons. For example: to get promotion, to move into management, to specialise (eg in testing or in ESP teaching), to get the chance to reflect on their experience and the theories it embodies.

The underlying theories behind language teaching and learning are focused on the first term of studies (autumn). In the second term, students choose from a range of options. In the third term, they may take further options – and thus complete the MA course in just nine months – or they do the research for a dissertation (and take a total of twelve months for the course). Alternatively, students may enrol on the distance study version of the MA TEFL, taking a longer period for their studies.

Teaching is by means of lecture, seminar, workshop, and internet discussion, with an emphasis on helping students reflect on and make sense of their experience.

Cambridge
Certificate in English Language Teaching to Adults

Commitment to excellence in ELT

The **Certificate in English Language Teaching to Adults** is an initial qualification for people who wish to become professional English language teachers. CELTA provides a thorough practical and theoretical introduction to English language teaching and is recognised by employers throughout the world.

Full- and part-time courses are available at over 200 centres in 38 countries.

For further information please contact:
Cambridge English Language Teaching
University of Cambridge
Local Examinations Syndicate
1 Hills Road
Cambridge CB1 2EU
United Kingdom

Tel: +44 1223 553789
Fax: +44 1223 553086
e-mail: efl@ucles.org.uk

www.cambridge-efl.org/teaching

"The course has been hard work but so enjoyable as every day offers something new. I finally feel like a teacher."
Radha Rajkotia

"I learnt so much in the four weeks that I now feel capable of tackling any class with confidence."
Cathy Radford

"Having the CELTA qualification gave me the ability and the confidence to change my life completely. I have come to realise that there are thousands of jobs in EFL and, with two years post-qualification experience, the world is my oyster."
Shirley Dockerill

UNIVERSITY *of* CAMBRIDGE
Local Examinations Syndicate

Contents

Introduction   1

1. **The state sector in Britain**   16
   Adult education; Teaching in schools; Further education
   colleges; Government-funded private training providers;
   Universities

2. **The private sector in Britain**   35
   Private language schools; Summer schools; Private
   tutoring; Home teaching; Young learners

3. **Teaching abroad**   53
   Volunteering; Private tutoring; In-company language
   teaching; Private language schools; Young learners;
   Universities

4. **Moving and working abroad**   75
   Sorting out the paperwork; Your contract;
   Accommodation; Learning the language; Settling in
   and making friends

5. **Initial qualifications in ELT**   93
   Introductory courses; ESOL-specific training; Distance
   learning certificates; UCLES and Trinity certificates in
   ELT

6. **Specializing and moving up the ladder**   108
   Young learners; ELT diploma courses; Postgraduate
   Certificate of Education courses; Moving on up

7. **Getting your first ELT job**   126
   Where to look; Voluntary Service Overseas; Your
   application; Preparing for the interview; The interview;
   Your first ELT job

8. **Related careers**   148
   Working in publishing; Translating; Dyslexia support;
   IT training; ELT recruitment

9. **Top tips for a successful career**   164
   Your first job; Planning lessons; Teaching; Teaching
   resources; The students; Getting support; Learning
   from experience; Working abroad

Glossary   173

Further information   175

Index   182

Introduction

Welcome to the world of English Language Teaching (ELT). There are lots of job opportunities within the field and this book will give you an overview of some of the possibilities and help you to work out the training you need to get the job you want. First, though, you need to find out whether ELT is right for you – are you the sort of person who will enjoy the job and do it well?

Is ELT right for you?

It is important to try to find out whether ELT is the right job for you before you start an expensive training course, change jobs or move abroad. There are many highly sophisticated tests and questionnaires that you can use to help you match your abilities and qualities to careers you are likely to enjoy. If you have not done one of these, then it might be a good idea to contact your local careers office and find out about what it has on offer. In the meantime, though, you might like to do this questionnaire to help you decide whether ELT is right for you.

Choose Yes/No for questions 1–5. Tick as many answers as you like for questions 6 and 7.

1. Do you enjoy meeting new people? Yes/No

2. Are you nervous talking to people you don't know well? Yes/No

3. Do you speak a foreign language? Yes/No

4. Do you like finding out about different cultures and ways of doing things? Yes/No

5. Do you enjoy trying to explain things? Yes/No

6. If you don't speak the language on holiday abroad, do you:
   a) speak English slowly and a bit louder and hope people will understand?
   b) learn at least 'please' and 'thank you' and point and smile a lot?
   c) use a phrase book and a dictionary to plan what you want to say?
   d) take the opportunity to learn as much as you can while you're there?
   e) assume you'll get by and guess as much as possible?

7. When you come across an English word you don't know do you:
   a) use the context to help you guess what it means?
   b) remember to look it up later?
   c) tune out of the conversation or stop reading because it's obviously too difficult?
   d) ask what it means?

1. Yes = 1 No = 0

2. Yes = 0 No = 1

3. Yes = 1 No = 0

4. Yes = 1 No = 0

5. Yes = 1 No = 0

6. a = 0, b = 1, c = 1, d = 1, e = 1

7. a = 1, b = 1, c = 0, d = 1

Check your answers. How did you score? If you got 10 or more, it is likely that you are the sort of person who would enjoy ELT. If you got a low score, it does not mean that you would not make a good English Language Teacher, but it does mean that you need to think quite carefully about what attracts you to ELT and whether you have got the mix of qualities and skills to enjoy the job.

Skills and qualities

It might be useful to look at what some experienced teachers think makes an effective English Language Teacher. Tick the skills and qualities that you think you already have and perhaps ask a good friend if they agree:

Qualities

▌ You need to be patient. (everyone said this)

▌ You need to be very creative and imaginative. (Sophia)

▌ You've got to be patient and very encouraging. (Cristine)

▌ You need to be very self-aware as, to be able to develop, you've got to realize where your faults are as well as your strengths. (Patrick)

▌ You need to be very culturally aware. (John)

▌ You need to have a global perspective on things. (Gary)

▌ You've got to be a team worker. (Keith)

▌ You need to be compassionate. (Andrea)

▌ You've got to have loads of energy and creativity. (Jo)

▌ You've got to have a sense of humour and an interest in the world. (Madeleine)

▌ You need to be open-minded. (Sean)

▌ You have to be sociable and diplomatic too. (Sophia)

▌ You need to be caring and reassuring and to have a lot of tact and diplomacy. (Andrew)

▌ You've got to be open-minded and have an ability to empathize. (Rachel)

▌ You've got to have tolerance and cultural awareness. (Sue)

▌ You have to be very open-minded and drop preconceptions about the Western way being the only way to do things and that we've got all the answers here in the West. (Sue)

▌ You've got to be patient and tolerant. (Rachel)

▌ You've got to be resilient. (Keith)

Personality

▌ You need energy and enthusiasm and to be fairly lively. (Ricky)

▌ You need to have an outgoing personality and to be quite friendly. (Andrew)

▌ You mustn't mind looking silly. (Paul)

▌ You've got to have the ability to put on a bit of a performance and be lively to get the students interested. (Miranda)

▌ You need to be reasonably outgoing and able to deal with a group of people. (Patrick)

▌ You have to be quite outgoing and energetic and willing to make a fool of yourself as it comes in handy in the classroom. (Aiden)

▌ You need a certain liveliness and vitality. (Annette)

▌ You've got to have a sense of humour and be able to use it appropriately. (Andrew)

▌ You've got to have an interest in the world an openness to people. (Madeleine)

▌ You need a sense of humour and a sense of fun. (Ricky)

People

▌ You've got to really like meeting new people. (Kate)

▌ You've got to have good people management skills. If you can't manage the class, it doesn't matter how good your knowledge of language is. (Sue)

▌ You have to like people and be interested in them. You have to be curious about what exactly moves them and about what possibilities there are in each person, as sometimes they don't even know themselves. (Sophia)

▌ You need to like people. (Andrew)

▌ You have to be able to feel for people and see them as individuals. (Liz)

▌ You've got to have a feeling for people from other cultures. (Ricky)

▮ You should be responsive and interested in people. It doesn't matter how good you are with the language and how many teaching techniques you have as if you haven't got a good rapport with the students then they won't get anything from you. (Nathan)

▮ You need to be able to encourage people and to be sensitive to them. (Ricky)

▮ You need to be responsive and interested in people. (Nathan)

Skills

▮ You need to have good organizational skills and an interest in the language. (James)

▮ You need to be very organized and be able to think ahead. (Andrew)

▮ You have to be able to really listen to your students. (Melanie)

▮ You need to be able to explain things again and again in different ways. (Alex)

▮ You've got to be flexible in the way you work and have common sense. (Miranda)

▮ You've got to be organized, systematic and have good time management skills. (Madeleine)

▮ You need to have a firm grounding of organization. (Nathan)

▮ You've got to be reasonably imaginative in the ways you present things. (Patrick)

▮ You need to have the ability to put concepts across and to listen. (Ricky)

▮ You need to be a good communicator and to like being around people. (Stella)

▮ You need to be able to listen and sound interested. (Pam)

▮ You've got to be able to motivate the students and understand their problems. (Andy)

Language

▌ You need to have a clarity of mind and an ability to see how language works and to analyse patterns. (James)

▌ You have to have an interest in the language. If you're not interested in the language, you're not going to make it interesting for your students. (Miranda)

▌ You've got to have a reasonable knowledge of grammar and language. (Rachel)

▌ You must be genuinely interested in language and how it works. (Roger)

▌ You have to have an analytical way of thinking to see that language is constructed in a particular way and there's a pattern. (Sophia)

Learning

▌ You've got to have a real desire that people should learn. (Ricky)

▌ You've got to understand the learning process and to care whether the students are learning. (Simon)

▌ You've got to want to carry on learning yourself. (Madeleine)

If you think that you already have a lot of these skills and qualities, then ELT might be right for you.

Good and bad aspects of the job

Like any job, ELT has its advantages and disadvantages and you will need to think carefully about what you like doing and the things that matter to you in your daily working life. People who stay in ELT generally agree about the aspects of the job that continue to give them satisfaction and tend to say the same things about the inspirations and rewards of the job as well as the irritations. This is what experienced teachers say about the best and worst aspects of ELT:

The best things

▌ It's very rewarding watching people develop, improve and achieve their goals. (Adrian)

▌ It's interesting. (Sean)

▌ The interaction with the students. (Azhar)

▌ The scope for creativity and the sheer variety of it. (Andrew)

▌ Meeting interesting people, both students from all over the world and fellow teachers. (Debbie)

▌ The rapport with the students and the sense of trust that begins to develop. (Steve)

▌ I like to think I've empowered people. I think that's great. (Cristine)

▌ You learn to feel at ease with other people who are very different from yourself. (Debbie)

▌ If it's going well you can see it. (Andrew)

▌ Meeting people from all over the world and helping them knock down the barrier of language. (Liz)

▌ Flexibility, travel and always being a little bit foreign and a little bit different. (Phiona)

▌ The challenge of making language learnable and making it interesting. (James)

▌ The feeling of progress and seeing people improve. (Andrew)

▌ You can enjoy yourself and have a lot of fun in the classroom. (James)

▌ I like the adrenaline and that feeling of performing and getting instant feedback about your performance. (Andrew)

▌ There's a great satisfaction when you see somebody's life turned around with some English classes. (Miranda)

▌ It's a nice feeling being able to help someone with something they need. (Andrea)

▌ The jokes, the laughs and the human contact. (Sarah)

I prefer working with people than with machines. I enjoy teaching because of the relationships. (James)

I love being in the class and the feeling when things are going right. (Jo)

The variety of students you find in your class. (Jo)

Being able to open up the pages of the *Times Educational Supplement* on a stressful and snowy day in England and to think, 'Now why don't I just go and work in Greece, Turkey, Japan etc.' (John)

Working with the students and getting to know the different personalities. I learn so much from them. (Nathan)

Meeting so many different people. (Josephine)

It's fun and it's interesting. (Sophia)

The ability to create, to generate and then to step back. (Andrew)

The fact that you can work anywhere in the world and get a good job. (Rachel)

You have a lot of autonomy in your subject and you can see people progress and pass exams. (Patrick)

It's interesting interacting with the students and you learn as much as they do really. (Rachel)

It's a people job and it's creative and varied. (Annette)

The flexibility of lifestyle. I enjoy the 'international passport' of having an ELT qualification and being able to just get a bag together and go. (Nathan)

There's so much variety. I have students from all walks of life and of different abilities, but they all want to learn. (Pam)

That every day's slightly different. (Rachel)

Everything's worthwhile when you're with the students and they suddenly understand a point. (Alex)

It's the students. The day I can't say that I'm leaving. (Gary)

You feel that you're really doing something worthwhile. (Ricky)

- The pleasure is in the relationships in the classroom and enjoying being there with the students. (Chris)

- The enthusiasm of the students. (Andy)

- Sharing the enjoyment of your students realizing they're learning. (Roger)

- Getting to know the students themselves as individuals. (Sophia)

- It's an incredibly engaging process and the whole of you goes into it. (Ricky)

- It's a challenge and it's not monotonous. (Patrick)

- You're usually teaching pleasant people who want to learn. (Annette)

- When you get a class that gets it, it's fantastic. (Ricky)

- It's satisfying seeing the way people progress over a period of time. (Alan)

- The students are lovely and they give you ideas. (Alex)

- The people that you meet and the fact that it's worthwhile. (Andrew)

- I like it very much. I can identify where people get blocked and it's nice to help them through that. (Simon)

The worst things

- The pay. (Sean)

- There's not really a worst thing. (Azhar)

- The pay and working conditions in some private EFL schools can be quite poor. (Debbie)

- Low pay and insecurity. (Phiona)

- It's quite intensive and you can do a lot of additional work at home. (Rachel)

- Paperwork. I hate it. It's increased a lot in the last few years and I'm not sure that all of it's necessary. (Sophia)

- The salaries and some of the working conditions. (Annette)

- The paperwork. (Patrick)
- Listening out for people's mistakes without hearing what they're really saying. (Madeleine)
- The time spent preparing resources. (Cristine)
- It's easy to be very self-critical. (Rachel)
- Management is the bane of my life. (Michael)
- It can be ghastly if you've got a group of unmotivated learners that are uncooperative as it's a lot of effort. It's like pushing a heavy cart uphill with the brakes on. But that's rare. (Ricky)
- The pay is not great. (James)
- The paperwork is easily the worst thing. (Gary)
- It's quite tiring as you have to be on show in a way. (James)
- There's a lot of paperwork and you're never going to get it quite right. (Andrew)
- There's always going to be something that you haven't done that you should do and that can be a bit stressful. (Andrew)
- The repetition of teaching the same thing and the students with the same types of mistakes. (Jo)
- The tendency to correct English friends at a dinner party. (John)
- The repetitiveness of it. (Keith)
- A lot of paperwork, which takes away from the teaching. (Aiden)
- The frustration when you can't do things you need to help people. (Miranda)
- The paperwork. There's just too much of it. (Nathan)

It is noticeable that teachers seem to find that the positive things easily outweigh the negative aspects of the job and to relish the contact with students and the feeling of doing something creative and worthwhile. Teachers complain about low pay and too much paperwork, but enjoy developing relationships with students and helping them learn. They also find their jobs interesting and fun and, if you think you would gain satisfaction from the same things, then ELT could be right for you. You will enjoy the job if human relationships are more important to you than money and if you like challenge and variety.

There are plenty of options available in ELT and different reasons for wanting to move into the field. For example, you may have just finished university and want a way of earning some money while living and travelling abroad, or you may be looking to do some voluntary work in your local community by helping local residents, asylum seekers and refugees who need to learn English. These are just two possibilities: you may want to do a bit of private teaching to supplement your income or you may be looking for a career change that allows you to be flexible about where and when you work. This book will give you the opportunity to find out more about the variety of ELT and to choose the training that will equip you to pursue the aspects of the work that interest you.

English Language Teaching today

For a variety of historical reasons, English is one of the world's major languages and is spoken as a first language not only in Britain, but also in Australia, New Zealand, Canada, the United States and parts of the Caribbean. It is also an official state language in India and Pakistan, large parts of Africa and Hong Kong. In addition, English is a worldwide language of business and trade and people all over the world recognize the need to learn it to enable them to communicate with their counterparts in other countries. People need and want to learn English, which means that there are plenty of opportunities to teach English both abroad and in Britain. You may teach in the state or private sector and you may work with adults or children, but whatever your interests there are lots of opportunities out there once you have decided the path you want to follow.

The field of ELT is very wide and its development and growth is rooted in history and politics, but it can be usefully divided into a number of fields, which are both separate and closely linked. It is important to understand some of the key differences between the fields, though, so that you can decide where and who you want to teach. ELT is an umbrella term, which covers all types of English Language Teaching, but there are some useful sub-divisions.

EFL/ESOL

Teaching English as a Foreign Language (EFL)

EFL means teaching English to people who are learning the language for pleasure, work or educational reasons. For example, you may teach EFL to au pairs living and working in Britain for a year before going back to their own countries to study further or to get a job. You may also teach business people who realize that they need English as the international language of commerce or you may have students who are studying English because they like the culture and enjoy English-language films and television. You may teach EFL in Britain or abroad, but the key factor about EFL is that the students are learning because they have chosen to for education, interest or work.

Teaching English for Speakers of Other Languages (ESOL)

ESOL means teaching English to people who live in Britain but speak a different first language or mother tongue as it is often called. For centuries, people from all over the world have come to live and settle in Britain for a variety of reasons. They may have been seeking a better life for themselves and their families or they may have been driven here by the fear of persecution or to escape danger and civil war in their own countries. All over Britain, there are communities of people who have settled here, but whose first language may be Turkish, Chinese, Somali or Urdu and who need to learn English to live, work, educate their children and participate in the community. You may teach young Kurdish teenagers in a further education college or you may work as a volunteer with Somali mothers with young families. You may teach long-term unemployed Bengali men or you may teach a mixed nationality adult education class, but the key factor about teaching ESOL is that people are learning the language so that they can not only survive in a foreign country, but also play an ongoing part in the economic, social and political life of Britain.

In other words, you can teach EFL in Britain or abroad, but you can only teach ESOL in Britain. Many teachers agree that the differences between EFL and ESOL are not significant and move between EFL and ESOL doing both, but others feel that the kinds of teaching are significantly different as the needs, interests and aspirations of the learners are so different. It is certainly initially important for you to think about where you want to work and the kind of students you think you may enjoy teaching.

ESP/EAP

Once you have worked in ELT for a while you may have the opportunity to specialize and to teach in industry, universities or for private organizations or businesses.

English for Special/Specific Purposes (ESP)

The specific purposes covered by ESP can be varied. A particular organization, for example, the World Youth Hostel Organization, may want its employees to be able to speak English for very specific purposes like taking bookings, greeting guests and dealing with complaints. You may be asked to tailor a course to fit these specific requirements. Usually the organization is clear about what it wants and needs and your job will be to design and deliver the teaching programme.

English for Academic Purposes (EAP)

There are many overseas students in Britain at colleges and universities and an EAP teacher might teach them the English they will need to study their specialism, for example, engineering, medicine or agriculture. In addition, some university students overseas will study their academic subjects in English and you may work teaching them the language they need. It is helpful if you also have some knowledge of the subject your students are going to be studying; for example, English for engineering, could be quite difficult for you to teach if you failed your physics and maths GCSEs and you probably would not enjoy it. Subject knowledge is not essential, though, and you will find that you learn lot about your students' subject while you are teaching them English.

Teaching adults or children

You will need to decide whether you are interested in teaching adults or children, as the training routes are generally different and you will probably also have a clear preference.

Adults

Teaching adults means working with people who have a wealth of experience about life, but also about language learning as they have already successfully learned their own first language and perhaps others. If you want to work with adults, you will probably enjoy meeting people from different cultures and backgrounds and exchanging information and ideas with them in the process of teaching English. You may teach:

▌ in Britain or abroad;

▌ in the private or state sector;

▌ one-to-one or in classes;

▌ EFL or ESOL.

The key thing about teaching adults is that the learners will have their own lives and interests and will generally have clear goals as well as their own ideas about how to learn and what they like and do not like doing in class.

Children

Teaching a foreign or second language to children or younger learners can be very rewarding as they are lively and tend to be fairly relaxed about making mistakes, which means you can do all sorts of fun activities in the classroom. As you can imagine, though, the regulations and requirements covering the teaching of children are fairly rigorous and, in many cases, you need to have qualified teacher status before you can get work.

Private sector

Much ELT with children is EFL either at short summer schools in Britain or in private after-school classes abroad. The children's parents will have decided that it is a good thing for them to learn English and will be paying for extra classes over and above those provided as part of the school programme. The summer schools usually include a full social programme and a variety of sports and other activities like drama so it helps if you can offer a specialism or some experience in addition to ELT skills.

State sector

Britain   English for the children of local residents and refugees in Britain is integrated into their normal mainstream schooling and classes will consist of children who speak English as a first language as well as those who speak it as an additional language. To teach English in British schools you need:

- a degree in a national curriculum subject;

- GCSEs in English and maths;

- qualified teacher status, which means a PGCE (Postgraduate Certificate of Education) or a BEd (Bachelor of Education).

Once you are qualified, there are additional specialist courses you can do that focus on ways of supporting bilingual children.

Overseas   In many countries, children learn English as a Foreign Language at school in the same way that children in Britain learn French or German. You may want to teach in an English-medium school or in the country's state sector, but again you will need to have qualified teacher status as a prerequisite.

In other parts of the world (often Commonwealth countries), English is one of the official languages and children at school will receive their mainstream education in English after the age of 11, so teaching English there is like teaching English as a mainstream subject rather than as a foreign language.

The following chapters will outline the full range of ELT possibilities in Britain and abroad and explain some key terminology so that you can find your way through the field and decide what sort of teaching you think you would like.

1 The state sector in Britain

The state sector in Britain offers the opportunity to:

▌ teach EFL, ESOL or both;

▌ work in further, higher or adult education or for a training provider;

▌ work as a volunteer ESOL tutor in adult education or for a community group.

There are advantages and disadvantages in each and you may try different sorts of ELT before you find something that suits you. Working in the state sector is better paid than the private sector, although you will not earn a lot in ELT.

Stella, who used to work in banking, and Steve, who used to work in insurance, are now both full-time language teachers and agree that ELT is 'about the quality of life in the end'. Stella says, 'You've got to have an enthusiasm for it. There have been situations in the past where I've hated going to work, but to enjoy going to work is worth a few thousand pounds.' You will teach a wide variety of students. Some will be permanent residents living and working here, others from Europe have the right to live and work here for a number of years and others will be in Britain to learn English and will then go back to their own countries and continue their studies or get jobs.

Adult education

The provision of language classes varies from borough to borough and is funded by the local education authority. Students do not generally pay fees, although they may be asked to pay a nominal amount, for example £15, to cover the costs of registration. Classes are part-time in local schools, church halls and other community buildings and Miranda, an ESOL organizer, says they hold classes in 'portacabins in sportsgrounds and playgrounds, in church halls and in the medical rooms of schools,' as 'We're community-based and the idea is to keep it local so we try to get people into a class near their house that's also at the right level.' The classes are usually timetabled to fit in with school hours so parents or au pairs can deliver and collect children from school and still attend class or they are held in the evening to cater for people working full-time. Some classes provide a crèche, although this is sometimes in the same room in which you are trying to teach so you must be prepared for interruptions and distractions, with excited or crying children competing with you for their carers' attention.

Because of the way in which adult education is funded, all students have to enter for some form of external accreditation. ESOL students often enter for qualifications that have national recognition and build up a portfolio of work over the year, while EFL students usually sit an examination, for example, Pitmans or Cambridge, which are recognized internationally.

The students

The ESOL students are usually studying part-time because they have children or are working, which means they have busy lives outside class and may not find time to do homework. As they are likely to be living with their families, they will speak their own language at home, so their opportunities to practise English outside class may be limited. The students' ages will range from 16 or sometimes even younger to mid-60s and you may get teenagers and grandparents in the same class. Some students may have lived here for many years, but others will be new arrivals and may need help and advice with practicalities like how to use public transport or how to register with a doctor. ESOL classes can be very empowering for students and Miranda says that, 'It's just amazing seeing people make progress and being able to help their children or resume careers they had before. It changes people's lives and opens up a whole new world for them. If they can't speak the language they're very isolated.'

Asylum seekers and refugees will probably have left their own countries in distressing circumstances and some may be quite traumatized by what they have experienced and seen, so you will have to be sensitive to this in class. Miranda explains that 'Although you don't want to become a counsellor or social worker, you've got to understand that people have got other things in their lives apart from grammar. Although it's important, there are times when they're not going to be able to concentrate because of other things going on in their lives.' She says that 'Many of the students are highly educated people who need to improve their English so they can get on and get back into the workforce.'

Others may have had their education at home interrupted by, for example, war or family disaster and may need to top up their basic education as well as improve their English. They may also need help with literacy skills, and adult education is often the first step in catching up on what has been missed. Adult education also takes complete beginners, which means they may not be able to write or even to answer the question, 'Hello. What's your name?', so you must be prepared to mime or point and to take things at a very slow pace. Miranda says that 'It's amazing how people manage to turn up at a class even though they can't speak a word of English. We publicize classes through libraries, medical centres and schools, but word of mouth is incredible and people get brought to us by neighbours, friends and relatives.'

The EFL students are likely to be studying part-time and many will be working, but they are unlikely to be living with their own families so they will get more chance to speak English outside class. Students tend to be in their late teens or early 20s, although there will sometimes be people in their 40s or 50s.

Some may be living with British families, if they are working as au pairs for example, but others may be living alone and be quite lonely, so making friends with other students is important. Most will be studying English because they want to pass exams that will help them continue their studies or with their jobs. They have usually already learned some English in their own country and have a good standard of education and fairly good study skills. The students are in class because they want to learn and are paying for themselves, so they are generally well motivated and prepared to work hard outside class.

Working conditions

Full-time teaching jobs in adult education are rare, although many boroughs will have a 'Language Organizer' who may be full- or half-time and paid during the holidays. Most adult education teachers are employed by the hour and, therefore, do not get paid for holidays. You would probably be offered up to 12 hours a week by a borough, though you could work for other boroughs as well and build up enough hours to make up a full timetable if you wish. Miranda's teachers include parents with young children, someone studying for an MA, a psychiatric nurse and someone who works in a theatre, so if you have outside commitments and responsibilities or do not want to work full-time for other reasons, then teaching in adult education may be ideal for you.

You must be prepared to teach at different venues in the borough, though, and to do your preparation and marking at home as you will not have a desk to work from. Miranda warns, 'Facilities and resources are often limited or may be kept at a different site from the one at which you teach, so you need to be prepared to make a lot of your own materials and take everything you need with you. You may be lucky and have a lockable filing cabinet in the classroom where you can keep a tape-recorder and dictionaries, but sometimes you might not even have that and have to carry everything with you to classes.'

Adult education generally has limited resources and students may be asked to pay for photocopies of materials you give them, but there will be some tapes, videos and books. Miranda says that 'Teachers spend a lot of time making their own materials and cutting, sticking and photocopying bits out of different books and magazines, trying to make things that fit the needs of their class. They're always thinking of their particular group of students and what they need and looking out for materials to use.' This may suit you if you are creative and enjoy producing things and trying them out.

In terms of teaching, it can be quite lonely as you may not see other language teachers if their classes are at another site. Andrea, who teaches part-time, says, 'If you're not careful you can become quite isolated,' but the advantage is that you will have a degree of independence and, 'To a great degree you're left to your own devices.' You will have the opportunity to get to know people in your neighbourhood as students usually attend classes at the site nearest to their home and often come back to classes for a second or third year. You must be prepared to bump into your students in the supermarket or post office at the weekend.

Volunteers

A good way to find out if ELT is for you, is to work as a volunteer teacher without giving up the day job. Adult education uses volunteers in classes with an experienced teacher as there are often students of different levels in the same group and it is useful to the teacher and helpful to the students to have another person in the classroom. Community organizations use volunteers because they are usually very short of money and are looking for ways to help their members on limited funds and with few resources.

Home tutors

Adult education also uses volunteers to work in people's homes. People may be taught in their homes if they cannot attend classes for some practical reason, for example, they have a disability or a number of small children and there is no crèche available. Teaching someone in their home can be very rewarding and Miranda, who began as a home tutor volunteer says that for her, 'It was a good start as it made me want to go on and do more. You get very much more involved with the students and get to meet all the family because they usually like to come and have a look at you. The children will come in from school and want to see how their mum's getting on or the mother-in-law will want to join in and you'll end up with two of them.'

You will not have any equipment like a board, though, and will have to make the most of what is there, as well as what you take with you, and do lots of oral work. Cristine also began her career as a home volunteer and explains that, 'It's nice for the students because they're comfortable and relaxed in their own homes and you teach them practical English for talking to their children's school and going to the hospital.' Teaching someone in their home is also a good opportunity to look at cultural aspects. People who have lived here a long time, but have only just started to learn English, may already know quite a lot about British customs, but for new arrivals everything will seem strange. Cristine says that her student, 'noticed I had a wedding ring and wanted to know about that and I asked them about their weddings and we shared cultural information'. You will probably be offered tea and will chat to the family before or after the class, which is a good way to get to know people from different backgrounds.

Classroom volunteers

As a classroom volunteer, you do not usually plan the lessons or teach the whole class, but you work with a small group or individual students who need extra help. Sue, who now trains ESOL teachers but began as a volunteer, says, 'The advantage of the system is that you get a really good idea of what it's like teaching ESOL.' If you work with a class, the teacher may use you to work with weaker students who need extra support or perhaps with an advanced student who is shooting ahead and getting the work done before everyone else. She says that, 'It's a matter of luck how much the class teacher allows you to do. It may be mainly one-to-one work or you may do activities with a group. If the teacher trusts you enough and is convinced you can hack it, you may be asked to prepare and deliver your own activities with some of the students or perhaps to take the whole class for part of the lesson.' It is useful to be able to watch an experienced teacher at work and you may find that you are happy to continue as a volunteer and do not want to go on to teach. You have the pleasure of working with students without the responsibility of preparing lessons and marking work.

You may want to work as a volunteer for a number of reasons; you may have retired, for example, and want to continue to use your skills without starting on a second career. You may be a mother with children at school, and want to do something part-time without having to make a full-time commitment or spend a lot of time on preparation and marking. Alternatively, you may see volunteering as the first step into teaching as a career and it may lead onto ELT training. Miranda's volunteers tend to be people who have travelled and find that they want a way to continue mixing with people from different cultures and with different languages or people who want to help the community and give something back.

Stella, who now teaches full-time in an FE college, had a lot of time on her hands while she was convalescing from an accident and responded to an advertisement for volunteers in her local paper. She knew almost nothing about language teaching, but 'went to the first class and just loved it and thought this is it. This is exactly what I want to do.' Most local authorities provide some basic training for volunteer ESOL teachers and many continue to work as volunteers while they are doing the next stage of training (see Chapter 5). Once they are qualified, many volunteers are then offered their own class and paid work by the organization for which they have been working, but this is not guaranteed and opportunities, particularly in community organizations, are often limited by funding.

Working for community organizations

You may want to help one of your local ethnic minority communities by offering your services as an English Language Teacher. Many community organizations include language classes in the services they provide for their members and these are often held in community centres. There are some opportunities for paid work if the organization has managed to get hold of some funding, but community groups are always in need of volunteers to help. Facilities may not be good (there may not be access to photocopying and there may be more than one class in the same room), but the students will live nearby and there will probably be a crèche.

Attending classes at a community centre may be the first step for learners who can then progress to more English classes at an Adult Education Centre or FE college or to vocational training, higher education or employment. Working with learners in your own community can be a very good way of giving something back and making a contribution. Aidan, who had travelled in South America and spoke Spanish, started by helping a South American self-help community organization by doing some translation for them and then did some teaching as a volunteer. 'I was thrown in at the deep end, but it worked. They had no facilities and there were kids wandering in and out all the time, but I had a friend who worked for a company in the city that changed their logo every five minutes and he gave me lots of notebooks and pens, which helped. It's give and take and I got a lot of experience out of it and they learnt English. They got a lot out of it and so did I.'

Teaching in schools

If you want to work as an English Language Teacher in schools in Britain, you must have a degree and qualified teacher status. You can also become a teacher via the Registered or Graduate Teacher Programme, which means you can work in a school as an unqualified teacher and be trained on the job while you are getting paid.

There are many children in schools in Britain who have English as an Additional Language, but they are taught in the same classes as other children. Simon, who was a primary school teacher before retraining as an EFL teacher, worked in east London where the majority of the children in his class spoke English as an Additional Language. At the time, he did not have any special language training, but was in a specially designated school that had small classes and he had the expertise so that, in the end, nearly half his timetable was teaching small groups of children who were new to London. They were 9-, 10- and 11-year-olds who 'were fluent in their first language, but had no English'. Children learn language very fast, though, and 'It's amazing that you get children coming in with no English and within a few months they're speaking it with a London accent and sound exactly the same as their mates.' The school will usually offer support with language and this takes different forms depending on the age of the children and the kind of help they need. If you are interested in supporting bilingual pupils in school, there are specialist courses you can do on top of your teaching qualification.

Further education colleges

Each borough has a further education (FE) college and these are usually large institutions offering full- and part-time courses in a very wide range of subjects. As in adult education, some colleges have separate classes for EFL and ESOL, while others put all English Language learners together. Colleges are funded by the government, which insists that all students must enter for accreditation and, as in adult education, the EFL students enter for external exams while the ESOL students usually do a qualification that includes an element of coursework.

Students enrol for at least a term, although many stay for a year and may come back for a second year. Sophia, who teaches ESOL full-time, says that the best thing is when you get to know the students. 'You get to know them as individuals and that's the most rewarding thing and it happens gradually. I really like the second term, because by that time the group of students has really gelled and you discover all sorts of different aspects of their personality.' Classes will be mixed nationality and can be anything from 15–25 students. They may be full- or part-time and can also be in the evening or on Saturday.

Students

ESOL students in further education colleges often have clear goals in terms of continuing their education and training to help them gain employment. Some will have already studied in adult education and progressed to higher level classes at a college, but others will have come straight into FE. Many will want to progress to other academic or vocational courses in the college when their English is good enough. Sophia, who teaches full-time, says that, 'You're doing more than just teaching them the language. You're giving people a chance to live a better life in a new country, particularly people who are disadvantaged like refugees.' The adult learners are usually highly motivated, but like any adults they will have lots of responsibilities and pressures and may find it difficult to find time or space to study outside class.

You may also teach classes of teenagers from places like Somalia or Kosovo and many of them will be living alone away from their families, so will need some pastoral support as well as teaching. Aidan, who teaches ESOL full-time in an FE college, explains that, 'The youngsters are over here on their own and their parents are thousands of miles away, if they know where they are. Teaching involves helping them develop as people, not just teaching them in the classroom.' Steve, who now teaches ESOL full-time, agrees that the pastoral element is an important part of the job, 'Obviously most of the involvement is concerning their language learning, but you have to be aware of where they've come from and you have to listen to the students. A sense of trust develops and I found out in the second or third term with one chap that his brother had been shot right next to him.'

They will also be lively and energetic like all young people and may need persuading to work, but Stella says, 'I love the challenge of teenagers. It's just great and I get a real buzz out of it.' They will also need help in deciding on career goals and the next steps to take in getting further education or training.' Sophia, who first trained as a secondary school teacher in Greece before coming to England and training for ELT, agrees that, 'It's really nice to see them develop, particularly the younger ones, because they change. I often see people I've taught three or four years ago and it's really lovely when people come back and tell you what they've achieved.'

The EFL students will be like those at private language schools, but fees at further education colleges are usually less than in private colleges and the students might have chosen to study there partly for that reason. Unlike private colleges where students can sign up for as little as a week, they enrol for at least a term and many stay for as long as a year, which means you get the chance to get to know them well. Patrick, who has taught in Italy and Iran and now works in Britain, says 'It's quite a challenge and never boring or monotonous as you have a change of students every term. You have a nice mix of students of different ages and nationalities and it's good as you can see people progress quite quickly and pass exams.'

Teachers tend to socialize less with their students than at private colleges, but the students get the chance to meet students doing other courses and to mix with native speakers, which is good for their English. The EFL students will generally have a good standard of education and will be learning English because they want to study it at university or because it will improve their job prospects at home. Classes will include students from all over the world, so they will have to use English to talk to each other as well as to you. Patrick explains that, 'It's easier to teach English to multi-lingual groups as they're forced to speak English to communicate with each other and they're also picking it up outside the classroom, so they progress more quickly.'

Language support

As well as doing straightforward ELT, you could also work doing 'Language Support' in an FE college. This means you would help the students with the English they need to succeed on their academic or vocational course, which might be anything from A level biology to an HND Hospitality and Catering. The aim of ESOL students in FE colleges is to learn enough English to get jobs or to progress to mainstream courses where they study in the same class as native speakers and get an academic or vocational qualification at the end of it. Colleges also take on overseas students to study courses like Art Foundation, Fashion, Hospitality and Catering or Childcare. It is recognized that these students will need extra help and support with their English and your job would be to liaise with the mainstream teachers to find out the language the students need to learn. This might be the specialist vocabulary of a particular subject like Pattern Cutting or Childcare or it might be linked to study skills and more formal ways of talking or writing about their subject.

The level of English support varies widely as you may support students on any course in the college from Foundation level to A level and above. Ricky worked with a class of first- and second-year HND Hospitality and Catering students wanting to progress to university to do a degree, while Jackie's students were struggling with the language of their City and Guilds Fashion course. Language Support is hard work as you usually have to develop and produce your own materials and Jackie spent a lot of time finding out about the Fashion course and making ELT materials. For it to work well, you have to work closely with the mainstream tutor and it can be difficult to find time to do this in a busy college. Jill, who worked with science students, says, 'I was always dashing round trying to catch the tutor between classes,' and it may be almost impossible if you are part-time. Language Support can be very satisfying, though, as the language you are teaching is always directly relevant to the mainstream course your students are studying and it is rewarding to see them make progress.

You may teach the students as a group or you may work in an English Support Centre where you might see students one-to-one by appointment or on a drop-in basis. Sometimes students are reluctant to take up the offer of Language Support so attendance can be poor. When the support is welcomed, you get to know the students well as you work with them for one or two years throughout their course. The most rewarding thing is seeing the students progress and succeed on their mainstream course. Jill says, 'I loved it when the results came out and a student who'd been really struggling because of their English at the beginning had actually passed and had good enough grades to go on to university.'

Social programme

There are usually some social activities organized for EFL students, but not as many as in private language schools. There tend not to be so many social activities for ESOL students because asylum seekers and refugees do not generally have the money to participate and religion and custom may limit participation in mixed sex parties or those that involve alcohol. You may take your students on a class trip to a museum at the end of term, but this will usually be in class time and will be educational as well as fun. There may be an end of term party for EFL or ESOL students, but teachers organize these in their own time. It might be part of your job to organize trips to places of interest like Bath or Windsor, but there may be only a couple of these a term and there is not usually a social organizer at an FE college.

John, who teaches EFL full-time at an FE college, arranges coach trips and occasional theatre excursions as part of his job and his wife Anna often goes with him to help out as it can be hard work marshalling a large group of lively EFL students in a strange place. She says, 'It can be quite a hassle contacting everywhere to check that they are open and that they'll let a large group visit. It's fun being with the students, but it can be tiring as a small group will usually stay with you the whole day, even if you've said they can wander off on their own for some of the time. You're exhausted when you get home, although you do have a good time with them.'

Summer schools

State colleges usually have EFL summer schools with classes in the morning. You may have a reduced teaching load during the year so that you are available to organize and teach at the summer school or you may do it as overtime. Teaching at a summer school course is a useful way to get experience as colleges usually take on additional temporary staff to work alongside experienced teachers. Schools are not residential, but there are usually some outings and picnics arranged and the atmosphere is different from term-time as the students are not working towards a qualification, so it is more relaxed. Andrew, who used to work in Israel, now works at an FE college and runs the summer school. He says, 'We organize a couple of social things a week, perhaps a pub visit and a trip somewhere, but it's not like being at a big language school and the students tend to do their own thing. The programme is much less structured too and tends to be theme-based, so teachers can do more of what they like.'

Training

Teachers working in FE will need at least an ELT certificate and many will have a diploma and a Certificate of Education as well. Teachers with a certificate will be encouraged to get a diploma and Steve, who has both says, 'There's almost a feeling that if you haven't got a diploma, why not? You'd be encouraged to do one and the college would pay all or some of your fees to do it part-time.' Some FE colleges run ELT diploma courses and you could study at your own college to do it or go elsewhere one or two evenings a week. The department in which you work will probably organize one-day training events on different aspects of ELT and you will discuss materials and issues at regular team meetings. Working as part of a team means that you have the opportunity to learn from more experienced colleagues and you will have the opportunity to teach at different levels and to develop your own ideas. You will also be able to apply for funding to attend conferences and training outside the college and may even get a contribution towards the fees for an MA in TESOL if you want to go on to do one.

If you do not have qualified teacher status and teach more than a couple of hours a week, you will be encouraged to do a teacher training course at your own college or one nearby and get the chance to study with teachers of subjects other than English. The college will pay for this and will usually give you some time off teaching for this if you are full-time. Colleges also have extensive staff development programmes offering short and long courses on subjects other than ELT, so you will have the opportunity to learn other things like desktop publishing, counselling or how to tutor online if you wish.

Working conditions

Teachers in FE can work full- or part-time and can be expected to teach up to two evenings a week with time off in lieu. If you work full-time, you will teach approximately 23–25 hours a week (the number of hours is recommended nationally, but varies slightly between colleges) and be paid during the holidays. Some people are employed on what are called fractional posts because they work a fraction of a full-time post and are paid in the holidays as well. Rachel, who worked in private language schools before getting a job in FE compares the two sectors and says, 'You get holiday pay and sick pay and a reasonable salary, so you feel that you're valued a bit more and that it's more professional. It depends where you're working, of course, but security is the biggest difference.'

Many teachers in FE work part-time and this is often the first step to a full-time post. Teachers need to be employed through an agency and have to register with one before they can get work and you can expect to earn around £13–16 an hour at the time of writing. Some teachers work part-time at more than one college to make enough money to live on and may have to travel between different college sites. When Stella first started, she worked at three different venues for two different boroughs. 'It's very hard because of the travelling and because you don't really belong anywhere and don't have a base. The good thing, though, is that the teaching I did at each site was so different that I got a really good grounding.'

Facilities at colleges are generally good and your students will probably have access to a library, computers and a language laboratory. There will be sets of coursebooks, readers and dictionaries available, although you may also order these and sell them to your students. You will have easy access to photocopying, cassette and video recorders, although you may also make some of your own materials. You will share an office, but have your own desk if you are full-time and have access to a shared phone and computers. Aidan, who used to work for a community organization and in adult education and now works in FE, appreciates the facilities. He says that, 'It's brilliant to have all the photocopying here as you used to have to go and pay to get material copied and then charge the students, which was a real hassle. It's also great to have e-mail and access to the Internet.'

If you get a full-time job in a college, there are different levels of responsibility, which means that there are possibilities for career progression. Rachel has found this, 'I think FE is better in terms of career because you have more opportunity for different things.' You may be responsible for organizing a particular course or a summer school or for testing students on entry and placing them in a class of the right level. You will be expected to attend school or department meetings on a regular basis and to work as part of a team. Teachers in FE all have to do a lot of administrative work in addition to teaching, as colleges are accountable to the public for the effectiveness of what they do. Colleges are regularly inspected by government agencies, but ELT departments also seek accreditation by The British Council or BASCELT (British Association of State Colleges in English Language Teaching), which look at management and administration, premises, resources, professional qualifications, teaching and welfare.

Government-funded private training providers

Another option as far as teaching ESOL is concerned is to work for a private training provider. These are private companies that are funded by the government to provide training to get people back into employment. They identify possible barriers to employment for people and offer training in subjects like numeracy, literacy and information technology for native speakers as well as ELT for second language speakers. The English is work-focused, so students can immediately see the relevance of what they are learning, and they can study other subjects in addition to English if they need to update other skills to help them get work.

The students

The students are a mixture of local residents, refugees and asylum seekers and are usually men over 25. Madeleine, who works full-time for a training provider after teaching EFL in Poland and at private language schools in Britain, says that, 'One student in 50 will be female, maybe 1 in 500.' Classes are free to students as they are government-funded, but there is an obligation to attend and students do not receive their job seekers' allowance if they do not go regularly. Madeleine says that it can be difficult teaching students who do not always want to be there and are only in class because they are frightened of losing benefit, but she finds the job very rewarding and loves the 'motivational, confidence-building aspect of the work and seeing the people in the room come alive'. Students leave the classes as soon as they find work, which, for some students, may not be for a long time and they could attend training for as long as a year.

Training

It is possible to get work for a private training provider without a formal ELT qualification if you have experience or other skills to offer such as teaching Basic Skills or IT. If you are not qualified, your employer will probably be prepared to make time for you to do a course and may even pay for it if you get taken on full-time. Madeleine, who already has an ELT certificate, was lucky enough to have employers who were interested in their staff's professional development and were prepared to pay for her to do an ELT diploma on a part-time basis.

Working conditions

You may get a full-time post, but most people are employed on short-term contacts and paid an hourly rate. A manager, who would prefer to remain anonymous, but part of whose job is monitoring the quality of private providers, says, 'The range of provision varies from the truly excellent to the mind-bogglingly appalling,' so be careful to check conditions of service if you are offered work. Madeleine reports that the hourly rate is not as good as in further or adult education, but that the salary is better than in private language schools. She has a full-time job and teaches for 17 hours a week, but has to attend meetings and carry out administrative duties for the rest of the time.

Staff turnover is often quite high and the aim is also for a high student turnover as people get employment, so you will be constantly meeting new people and forming new working relationships. You could also be quite isolated working for a training provider, as you may be the only ESOL teacher, so have no one with whom you can share ideas. The advantage is that you will probably have a lot of autonomy and be able to plan your own course and tailor it to meet your students' needs.

The work is demanding as you are under pressure to enable your students to learn enough English to find work and your employer will have employment targets to reach to ensure that they continue to receive government funding. As Madeleine says, though, 'It can be brilliant to help turn someone's life around by helping them get a job.'

Universities

Universities in Britain are increasingly keen to attract overseas students to study as they pay large sums of money in fees. Overseas students may be studying for first degrees or postgraduate qualifications or diplomas. Most universities with large numbers of overseas students offer various kinds of support with English and you will be teaching at fairly advanced levels.

The students

The students come from all over the world and will already have studied English in their own countries so you will not be working with beginners. They will have a high standard of education and be highly motivated and hard-working as they and their families will be paying very large sums of money for them to study in Britain. Some might be quite lonely as their families are a long way away and it might be difficult to make friends with English speakers as they often live in accommodation for overseas students and only meet British students in lectures.

Foundation courses

Some universities offer a one-year foundation course for students who need an additional year of education to get them to degree entry level and who also need to improve their English. They then can progress to a degree course. Ricky, who has taught in Spain and China, now has a fractional appointment teaching English and study skills for overseas students and spends a lot of time preparing and adapting materials. 'I enjoy it because it's at a high level and the students work really hard and are motivated. It's nice when you meet the students later and they're doing well on their degree courses.'

Pre-sessional courses

Some universities offer short intensive language courses before students start their programme of study. These pre-sessional courses run over the summer and students may study for one, two or three months. Universities often employ extra staff to teach on these courses and provide accommodation at the university. Students may be going on to study anything from engineering to art and your job will be to teach them the English they will need to study their specialism. Chris, who worked in Indonesia, taught on a pre-sessional course the year before and the year after he did his Masters and the classes included a mixture of General English and English for Academic Purposes (EAP). 'We all worked hard as we taught five hours a day, but there was a good social atmosphere as the teachers were all living at the university as well and we got to know each other quite well. The students were highly motivated and really serious about improving their English as they wanted to make sure it was good enough to study for their masters or PhD.'

On-course support

Many universities provide English support classes, which are tailored to the students' academic specialism (see EAP) and it can be useful, although not essential, if you have a background in the subject. You will often work quite closely with the lecturers for a particular subject and can find yourself learning a lot about science or engineering as well as teaching English. It will be more interesting for you if you are genuinely interested in the subject your students are studying, but it is not essential as your job is to teach English. Kate, who taught Bangladeshi postgraduates studying agriculture, says, 'I learnt more about rice crops and pests than I really wanted to know, but the students were lovely and were very enthusiastic about improving their English as they needed it for their course. They wanted to go back to their country to use what they'd learned to improve crop production.'

Working conditions

It is unlikely that you would work in a university as your first job and you would generally need to have at least an ELT diploma level qualification and some universities ask for a Masters degree in TESOL or Applied Linguistics. Pre-sessional programmes are short courses full-time over the summer and you may teach 25 hours a week and spend additional time doing preparation and marking. The hourly rate is often as much as £25 an hour, which is much better than further or adult education, but you will be employed on a short contract for one, two or three months and may live in student accommodation at the university.

There are some full-time ELT jobs in universities, but you usually need to have at least an MA and many advertisements specify that you should have or be working towards a PhD. Full-time teachers at university teach far fewer hours than in further education, so you have more time to prepare lessons and to mark students' work. It is more likely that you would be employed part-time or as a fractional appointment. Facilities and resources are generally very good and you will have an office, which you may share with two or three other people, a phone, a computer and good access to materials and photocopying. The students will be highly motivated by the desire to gain the qualification for which they are studying.

2 The private sector in Britain

If you want to work in the private sector in Britain, you will be teaching EFL and you have the choice of working for a language school or being self-employed and making your own arrangements to find students to teach privately. There tend to be lots of schools in the large cities, as well as tourist centres like Bath, Windsor, Brighton and Oxford and Cambridge. The large chains of language schools, like International House and The Bell, have a number of centres in Britain as well as abroad and working conditions tend to be good with opportunities for staff training and development.

There are plenty of very good privately owned small schools, too, but there are still some 'cowboy' operators as anyone can open a language school. Laurence, who had some ELT experience but no qualification, got a job with a small residential school on the south coast at which conditions went from bad to worse. The teachers and domestic staff were paid badly, then late and then not at all. Many staff left and those that remained tried to hold things together for the sake of the students. Laurence remembers that, 'The cook walked out one evening and I ended up doing the cooking for everyone, so at least we got something to eat.' He suspects that, 'It was a visa-laundering operation as nobody there seemed remotely interested in teaching. In the end the owner, who was a mad alcoholic, went bankrupt so I didn't get paid.' As with language schools abroad, the quality can vary, so it is wise to make sure that The British Council or ARELS (Association of Registered English Language Services) inspect and accredit the school if you want to work somewhere reasonable.

Private language schools

It is possible that you will get work at a private school in Britain without a recognized ELT qualification, but usually only if you have already had some experience abroad or have another relevant teaching qualification. Rachel, who had done a little teaching in Spain during her year abroad as part of her degree, had an interview at a school one day and started teaching there the next and Madeleine taught in Poland without a qualification and was offered a job in a small language school when she came back to Britain. This is not common, though, as English teachers are not in short supply and a certificate-level qualification is usually the minimum required (see Chapter 5 for advice about qualifications).

Teaching at a private language school can be interesting and stimulating as there will always be new students and teachers coming and going and classes running at different times during the day. Rachel says that the best thing about working in a busy school is that, 'Every day is slightly different.' Sean is in his 20s, has an ELT certificate and now works at a busy language school in central London. He says, 'It's really interesting meeting lots of people from absolutely everywhere.' He also says that he likes, 'being quite autonomous while I'm working. I don't have someone standing over me in the class all the time and I can make my own decisions. We have fun in class and I enjoy that.'

The students

Private language schools in Britain are attended by foreign language learners rather than local residents and refugees. Students come from all over the world and you will teach classes with a wide mixture of cultures and languages. You may have students from Brazil, Italy, Japan, China, Poland and Thailand in your class and everyone will have to use English to communicate. Classes tend to be small, between 8 and 12, and students will be at the school for anything from a week to a year either full- or part-time. Many schools now offer continuous roll-on enrolment with new students joining your class very week, so planning can be quite difficult, as you do not know who will be in your class the following week. Many students will be working towards examinations and these are often taken in December or June, but students can enrol for as long or as short a time as they like and are under no pressure to get qualifications.

The students are usually very motivated as they have made the effort to come over to Britain to learn English. Generally they will be here on their own and some may find it difficult to meet British people and make friends, so it is important for the teacher to help students get to know each other and make friends in class as they may feel quite homesick and lonely. Rachel thinks that it is an important part of the teacher's job to, 'help the students relate to each other on a personal level. Often they come with a lot of prejudices as they're not used to mixing with people from different cultures and backgrounds, so you need some way to help them work together.' Andrew, who teaches in north London says about his students, 'They're moneyed and their reasons for coming to Britain are cultural as well as educational. They're from a very wide background and their average age is about 22 or 23, although we do have people in their 60s.' They will not all be wealthy, though, and some students will be working to pay their way and may be au pairs or working at a local pizza restaurant, which means they will hear lots of English outside class and may even have English friends.

Business English

Lots of schools also offer Business English classes and these could be one-to-one or small groups. Classes will probably consist of learners in their late teens or early 20s studying Business English before going back to their own countries to continue their studies, perhaps by doing a specialist business or management course. They could also be studying general English as well in preparation for an exam that will enable them to do a course at a British college or university. There are plenty of good Business English materials available to use and, as the students will have little experience of the business world, you will be teaching some general business principles as well as teaching English.

Many schools provide one-to-one Business English lessons for business people and big multinational companies often pay for their staff to come to Britain and study intensively for a week or two. Alan works in London for a very large organization with schools all over the world and part of his job is to organize, 'highly intensive one-to-one programmes for professional business people. They're usually directors of their companies, but we've had actors, senators and football managers and people like that who very much need English. There are plenty of materials available for this, but you will also be expected to tailor your lessons to the requirements of the particular student and their particular area of business.' Rodney worked as an accountant for 30 years before teaching Business English and found that, 'The best thing about teaching English, as opposed to being an accountant, is the freedom one has to depart from a prepared lesson to meet students' special needs.' Alan says that tailoring the teaching to the student's needs is crucial and explains, 'We organize it in such a way that they feel important. They live in an environment in which they are considered important, so we make sure that they get that sort of experience here.'

Rodney's own business experience was invaluable as he taught students how to use the specialist vocabulary of banking and insurance. He usually taught senior executives, who wanted help with the language of business and accounting. Their English was already at quite a high level and they were usually very clear about what they needed to learn. In fact, he was offered more work than he could take on and Roger, now Director of Education at International House, Barcelona, says that age and experience are a great advantage for Business English. 'You can't send some 22-year-old in jeans and a T-shirt into a big company as it doesn't look right.' If you have an area of expertise from a previous career, then you can easily build on this and will have no difficulty in finding work teaching Business English. Some schools specialize in this and others include it as part of a range of courses on offer.

Social programme

Schools will have a social programme and it may be your job to help organize this. It could include visits to places of tourist interest as well as discos and social activities at the school itself. You will probably be expected to participate in some of these without being paid, although at Andrew's school, temporary teachers get paid extra to attend social events in the evening or at weekends. As he explains, 'Some of the events are very, very enjoyable. If you like your students it's a fun way of earning some extra money. For example, you can have a trip to Oxford and meet some friends there and not only is it free, but you get paid for it.' It is also an opportunity to get to know your students outside class and to chat with your colleagues.

Organizing the social programme can be interesting as you get the chance to get to know people from other cultures outside class. Part of Andrew's job is to organize the social programme as well as teach. He arranges a wide variety of activities, including 'discos, international food evenings, quizzes, football and other sports activities, all sorts of parties and competitions as well as a summer fair and a Christmas panto'. There are also trips to the pub and he puts on three or four events a week in the summer when there are lots of students. This can be fun, but it means he works two evenings a week, which would not suit everyone.

Andrew also organizes excursions to places like Oxford or Greenwich. He has to publicize the trips, book the coaches, collect the money and make sure he is covering the costs and go with the students for the day, usually a Saturday. He enjoys this as he is very sociable and it is a good way to visit some interesting places, but it can be quite tiring as you are with the students all day and have to make sure that you go home with the same number you started with. Michael, who organizes the social programme at his school, says that, 'Even though they are adults, losing a student is every teacher's nightmare. You're never sure whether the missing student is just late back for the coach or whether you should start getting worried in case something terrible has happened. I've never actually lost anyone, but I've had some anxious moments.'

Many schools also have their own newspaper or magazine and Andrew runs his school's newspaper, which means he not only writes articles himself, but edits contributions from students and other teachers. These may be jokes, letters, puzzles or stories and they provide valuable English practice for the students whether they are reading or writing them, as well as helping to create a sense of community in the school. Teachers at Sean's school also produce a free magazine and have persuaded local pizza places and coffee shops to advertise in it, which covers the costs of production. Sean contributes regularly to it. Students who have left often write letters to teachers and old friends and current students may write up a day trip or reviews of films or concerts.

Training

Most of the larger schools offer a staff development programme and may set aside a session a week where all staff get together for a short talk or presentation on an issue concerning language teaching. Neil, the Director of Studies in a school that is part of a large chain, 'organizes seminars for staff to exchange and discuss ideas', and this is very useful as it means you carry on learning and sharing ideas with other teachers and you can pick up some good tips. The larger publishers visit schools to promote new coursebooks and well-known ELT authors may come and do a talk and perhaps give away free copies of their latest book. At International House in London, for example, there are staff development sessions for people working there as well as regular talks and workshops on a Wednesday evening which, for a small fee, are open to teachers from other colleges as well. There is the chance of a drink and chat after the talk as a glass of wine is included in the price, so it is a good way to meet other teachers and to keep up to date with developments in the field.

International House also organizes an annual weekend conference in February, which is attended by staff from its schools all over the world, as well as teachers from both the state and private sector in Britain. There is usually a keynote address by an internationally known ELT writer or academic and then a choice of workshops and talks for the rest of the weekend. There is a wide variety of speakers and topics and the chance to exchange ideas with other teachers and trainee teachers; the food is usually excellent too and the conference is also a good way to keep in touch with old colleagues. Patrick, who has worked in the private sector and now runs the EFL department in a further education college says, 'The conference is brilliant as I catch up with all the old friends I used to teach with and get to meet people from other centres as well as putting faces to famous names in the field.'

Some schools deliver recognized ELT qualifications themselves and you will be encouraged to progress up the qualifications' ladder and to study for a diploma. Andrew explains that, 'I need the diploma if I'm going to make this my career. It's something I have to do. In schools that are recognized by the British Council and are progressive, you need a diploma to get a permanent position or to move up.' Your school may be prepared to support you with some time off teaching or will at least arrange your timetable to enable you to attend a part-time course at another college and they may contribute towards the fees for your diploma after you have worked for them for a while. Both Andrew's and Sean's employers are paying their diploma fees, so obviously have a real commitment to developing their staff, which is good for the school, but also good for you if you want to progress.

Working conditions

A full-time job usually means teaching about 25 to 28 hours a week and may include evenings. If this is your first ELT job and you are working at a good school, you will be given plenty of support and may not teach all those hours although you will be paid for them. Roger, who was Director of Studies at International House London for a number of years, says, 'Typically in our schools, we employ people on a 25-hour contract and we pay them for that, but we don't expect them to teach 25 hours. They'll teach half or three-quarters of that and the rest of the time they'll be with a Director of Studies helping them plan lessons. The amount of time they're teaching goes up as they seem able to cope.' Sean teaches at a school in central London and says that, 'The best thing about the job is the supportive atmosphere,' and Ricky remembers that in her first job she, 'had a great DOS who taught me a lot'. In a good school, you will find that the Director of Studies and other teachers will be very willing to share ideas and give you support, so make the most of help available to you and do not be afraid to ask questions.

There are many students who study all year round, but there is a seasonal element to ELT and there are always more students in Britain around Easter and a lot more in the summer. Because of this, many teachers are paid by the hour and Rodney taught on an hourly-paid part-time basis at three different schools when he first started. He ended up being offered more hours than he could manage, so it is important to decide how much you can cope with and learn to say no. Of course, you need the money, but there is a limit to how many hours you can teach and if you are travelling between schools you need to think about your travel time too. Rachel, who started teaching in the private sector, advises, 'Start gradually and don't be too ambitious in terms of the number of hours if that's possible.'

As a newly qualified teacher in your first job, you might be employed on an ad hoc basis and may be taken on for two or three weeks at a time for 15 hours a week teaching mornings or after-noons. This can be ideal when you are starting out and, when Andrew first began, he taught in one school in the morning and at others in the afternoon. It was, 'a nice little niche that allowed me to make every mistake in the book without getting penalized for it. The money was awful, but it suited me as I was learning.' Other teachers are employed for three months at a time and, because of employment law, are eligible for paid holiday after every 13 weeks of work. Some staff are on full-time permanent contracts, but others are on a yearly contract, which means paid holidays, but no security of employment. Annette, who works in ELT recruitment, admits that, 'Most people have to work for three or four years before they get a full-time contract.'

Pay in ELT is not good and Annette says that, 'It's badly paid considering that most people are graduates and that they pay for the training themselves.' Juliet McShannon reports in *The Guardian*'s *Education Supplement* (17/7/01) that an EFL teacher's starting salary on a yearly contract is approximately £14,250 and Annette, who was Assistant Director of Studies at a school in London, agrees that, '£14,000–15,000 would be the starting salary in London even after three or four years of experience.' As Sean says, 'The worst thing about the job is the pay, so don't think of going into ELT if you hope to get rich.' You can earn nearer £20,000 when you have gained some experience and if you take on additional responsibilities like organizing the school's teaching resources or the social programme, but it may take some time before you are in that position. The salary stretches further outside London, of course, and is subject to a yearly review, but most language schools are in big cities, seaside towns and tourist centres, which attract foreign visitors as well as language learners, so rents and house prices tend to be high. The low pay may be one of the reasons that EFL is often thought of as a job for young people in their 20s and Andrew, who has two young children, loves his job, but suspects that, 'The money will be the thing that will stop me teaching.' There is not a union for EFL teachers in the private sector and the only one willing to accept them is the General, Municipal and Boilermakers Union, which does not really meet the needs of the profession.

There is unlikely to be an overhaul of EFL teachers' pay structure, which varies from school to school and, in many of the bigger schools, there is a high staff turnover. In Jamie's school, for example, he has been there for 18 months and is the longest serving member of staff out of the 20 or so who work there and only his Director of Studies and Assistant Director of Studies have been there for longer. Because of this turnover, private language schools are usually lively places to work as the staff are often in their 20s or 30s and there is a good social life that goes with the job. Students and teachers might go for a coffee or to the pub after class and there is often quite a 'buzz' as there are always new staff and students and everyone is keen to make friends quickly and willing to join in things and have fun. The atmosphere is often lively and the pace fast, so this will suit you if you enjoy variety, stimulation and meeting new people.

Facilities vary, but large schools are usually very well equipped. At smaller schools, you may not have a language laboratory, for example, but you will have access to a photocopier and good schools will have a whiteboard, overhead projector, tape-recorder and video in each classroom. There will usually be a resources room, which may be in the same room as the staffroom, with copies of coursebooks, teachers' books, dictionaries, games, readers, cassettes and videotapes for you to use. In most schools, there will be someone whose job it is to organize the resources, copy tapes for you, record TV or radio programmes and order coursebooks for you to sell to the students. You will usually follow one course-book with your students, but will be expected to supplement it with other activities that you have taken from other sources or have devised yourself. Classrooms can be small and cramped, but there will be the opportunity to create wall displays of your students' work and there will be noticeboards advertising school trips and activities.

Staffrooms are often small and you will probably have to share a desk, so it will be difficult to find somewhere to work quietly as:

▮ Students will be knocking on the door.

▮ Teachers will be rushing around photocopying materials and trying to find the right place on tapes or videos they are going to use.

▮ The phone will be ringing.

▮ Teachers will be talking to students or each other.

You will probably find that you do most of you preparation and marking at home in the evening or at weekends as space is at a premium in most private schools.

Summer schools

Working in a summer school is a good way to get teaching experi-ence as soon as you have qualified, as schools take on lots of extra staff for Easter and the summer period. The big schools will offer two-, three- or four-week courses and students often combine studying with some sightseeing. Classes might be in the morning only to allow for this, but at other schools you will teach five hours a day and there will be trips to places of interest at the weekend. Steve, who is now a full-time ESOL teacher, got a job on a two-week summer school for Japanese students as soon as he had finished doing his ELT certificate course. 'It was hard work, although it was also fun as the atmosphere was very relaxed.' At his school, Andrew organizes three or four social activities a week for the summer students, which, 'allows parents, the people who are paying for the courses, to feel that their children are having a cultural experience as well as an educational one'.

Residential summer schools

Courses are sometimes residential as well and staff and students take over an established Oxford college or private boarding school for a month or two. Students can get very attached to each other as they live and work together quite intensely for a short period and there will probably be whirlwind romances as well as friend-ships. Laurence, who used to be a secondary school teacher, worked at summer schools in Eton and Hastings and says, 'There would be lots of tears at the end, which was quite funny really as they were for people they hadn't known three weeks earlier.'

Some of the teachers live in at a residential summer school and student-type accommodation will usually be provided at the school or college. A good way to get some ELT experience is to work as a Residential Tutor. Your job will not be to teach, but you will organize a full social programme. Marie worked as a co-tutor at a month-long summer school in Wimbledon and found that she enjoyed working with foreign language learners, trying to com-municate and meeting people from different cultures and she then went on to do ELT training. 'I spent all my time with the students when they weren't in class and didn't really get any free time because there was a lot to organize. We had football matches, a folk evening, a revue-type thing, which the students put on, and the usual pub crawls, discos and outings. The students were there to have fun as well as learn, so everyone went to bed really late and then they'd have to be up for classes in the morning.'

You will also have be on hand to deal with students' problems and queries. These can be anything from broken hearts to broken legs or might be something much more straightforward like how to use a public phone or where the nearest bank is. It is useful, but not essential if you speak a foreign language and Linda, whose degree was in French and German, worked as a Residential Tutor just after graduating and her French was extremely useful when one student lost her passport. She and her co-tutor lived in the same blocks as the students and one or both of them was always available. 'The students were great and we had a really good time, but it was absolutely shattering as you were always on call really and students were always asking you things. One knocked on my door at 6.30 am to ask for a sticking plaster for a tiny little cut he had. I could have killed him.'

Private tutoring

Anyone can advertise themselves as a private tutor and you can teach in your home or the student's. You do not need a qualification, but it will be easier for you and fairer to the students if you have some idea of what you are doing. There are things to be careful about (see advice in Chapter 3), but it can be a flexible way of working and give you valuable teaching experience. It can also suit you if you want to work part-time because you have small children or you have retired. Jill had an ELT diploma and advertised in the local paper when she took early retirement from further education. She initially took on two or three students who were studying at the local college and wanted extra help with their English. She charged £15 an hour, which seemed to be the going rate, and this worked out better than hourly paid part-time work in FE as she had no travel time or costs.

Connie, does not have an ELT qualification, but taught part-time in a private college for many years and still had contacts who referred students to her when she retired. She taught privately for about four hours a week and welcomed the extra income, which was tax-free, to supplement her pension. She is now 80 and suffers from arthritis, but still cannot completely give up ELT and teaches English to a Chinese neighbour in exchange for help with the garden and some shopping. 'She comes round to my house with her little boy and we have general conversation about things she's seen on TV or heard. I try to help with pronunciation or with any letters or forms she's been sent and we've also got a book that we use. It's difficult because the little boy wants to play all the time, but I look after him while she mows the lawn or whatever.'

Some language schools are happy to refer students that want one-to-one tuition to teachers who take on private students and they can make their own arrangements with them. Jane, who worked in a language school, gave extra private lessons to some South American students in her class and the school was quite happy with this. She says, 'They lived quite near me and I went to their house for a couple of hours a week on a Saturday afternoon. They were a husband and wife in my class and they were very keen, so I did it for a couple of months till they moved up to the next class. I did work quite hard preparing, but the extra money was nice.' You could also register with one of the private tutoring agencies, which will pass students to you, but they will take a fee for doing this and you will not make as much money as if you advertise yourself. If you have a particular expertise, you might create a niche for yourself offering private English lessons to learners involved in your own line of business.

Home teaching

Many EFL students live with families when they study in Britain and this may be a route into teaching for you if you have students staying with you and find you enjoy the experience of living with and getting to know people from other countries. Some students want to live with a family and have lessons at home as they think this will be the quickest way to improve their English. If you would like to try this, then you can advertise yourself offering accommodation and private teaching.

Gwen and her husband Michael live in a large house in a rural part of Ireland and started by taking two or three learners at a time. They put advertisements in newspapers abroad and produced a publicity leaflet, which they gave to the local tourist office. They offer full board and Gwen teaches in the mornings. She did not have any experience before she started, but took advice from a friend who had an ELT qualification and bought some good books and other materials. Her students generally come for a week or a fortnight and tend to be men who want to enjoy the opportunities for golf or fishing in the area. The enterprise has been successful and they have recently refurbished one of their outhouses and converted it into two study bedrooms with en suite bathrooms, so they can take on extra students. They have students throughout the year, but tend to get more in the summer and have now taken on an ELT qualified teacher who lives nearby and is glad of some extra work a few hours a week.

You can also register with one of the companies that organize home teaching for foreign language learners. If you apply through a company, it will come on an inspection visit to make sure that the house is clean and comfortable and that the room you are offering is of a reasonable size and has a bed, desk and wardrobe and so on. If you want to teach as well as offer accommodation, then you usually need a degree (this does not have to be in English) or a teaching qualification of some kind. Jan, who has been teaching students living in her home for more than 10 years, gets a lot of support from the company with which she is registered. It provides a coursebook, wallcharts and pictures, and guidance notes for teachers. This kind of work may suit you if you have other commitments and want to be able to work from home. Jan, whose children were still at school when she started, found the flexibility ideal and says, 'It meant I could work without having to face a traffic jam every day and I could fit in things with the family if one of the children was ill.' Students usually come for two or three weeks on a package that includes lessons for two, three, or four hours a day and they will expect to be taught rather than just have a chat with you. Most learners will have an intermediate level of English and it is unlikely that you would have to cope with a beginner who can speak hardly any English at all. The student will expect the lessons to be uninterrupted, though, so you will have to put on the answerphone and may have to persuade the children to turn down the television while you are teaching.

The disadvantage of teaching from home like this is that you cannot leave the job behind at the end of the lessons as the student is living with you and will expect to be part of the family and join you for three meals a day. Jan says that most of her students are adults and fairly independent but, 'Some only feel secure when they're with you and want to be with you every minute of the day. One never went out and would sit and watch TV with us every evening, so we never had any privacy.' This is not usual, though, and having students in your home may be a good way to meet people from other cultures and to get some experience of ELT.

You have to be flexible and willing to share your home and to be accommodating when students want to bring their own food from home and keep it in your fridge. Jan says that you have to be tolerant and, 'welcome the students and treat them as a friend coming to stay', and she has kept in touch with some students and they exchange letters and Christmas cards. Providing accommodation and teaching as well could suit you if you have a young family or if you work part-time and want to do something else without having to make a long-term commitment. The work is intermittent and, so long as you have a good-size spare room, you can take students to fit in with other things you are doing.

Young learners

Teaching young learners is a rapidly growing area of ELT and there are plenty of opportunities for you to gain experience working with children and teenagers. Most classes with young learners will be during the holiday periods at Easter or Christmas, but there are some Saturday schools in areas like London, which have a high proportion of foreign language speakers working in Britain for a period of time long enough to bring their families with them. Rachel gave private lessons and taught in a Saturday school and found that the key thing about working with young learners is, 'You need extra activities all the time and you need to change activities more often than you would with adults.' You need lots of energy and enthusiasm and, most importantly, you need to like children.

Children's summer schools

Lots of schools offer residential summer programmes for young language learners. An ELT qualification may not be essential, but you will need qualified teacher status or experience of working with children. Tony, a very experienced teacher now owns his own school, which runs residential courses for children. He says, 'We like teachers to have the CELTA or Trinity (see Chapter 5) and ideally they'd have a PGCE as well because this means they know all about taking children on trips and counting them and bringing the same number back.' If you want to teach at a summer school for young learners, it is essential that you like children and that you enjoy working with them. It is also useful if you can offer some kind of additional skill or ability like sport, music or drama on top of your ELT experience. Tony says, 'Basically, we're looking for a guitar-playing, clog-dancing football referee,' and he does find them.

Teaching young learners is very different from teaching adults and Katie, who teaches at residential summer schools in Brighton, says that, 'It's very enjoyable as you can do more fun things and there's more scope.' It is important to remember that children also have a shorter attention span than adults, so you will need to, 'have a big variety of things to do like games, songs and puzzles and you can't do anything for too long as they'll get bored'. The lessons are usually fun and Melanie, who has taught children in Britain and abroad, says that the best thing about teaching young learners is, 'their enthusiasm and unpredictability. They keep you on your toes and they keep you fresh. The range of activities from craft to music makes sure that teaching remains a learning experience for the teacher.'

The fact that the lessons are fun does not mean that you do not have to work hard and Melanie, who now trains teachers of young learners, says that, 'The most challenging thing is that you have to be well prepared – not opening the book at the next page stuff.' You will probably spend a lot of time planning lessons and activities to keep the children interested and cooperative. Rachel says that she, 'had to do lots of preparation looking for different things and I made sure I always had something extra up my sleeve in case they got fed up'. Melanie, says that, 'Children have wonderful enthusiasm and curiosity and can be fired up learning, but they also let you know when they are bored or when they don't like something, which is really good for a teacher.' She says that, 'You have to be adaptable in the lesson. If something isn't working, it has to be changed there and then.'

The students are in Britain on holiday, but they are also there because their parents have sent them to learn. John has organized a number of summer courses and says, 'Motivation can be a problem. Parents are happy to get rid of the kids for a month and the kids see it as an opportunity to go mad because mum and dad aren't around. They've broken up for summer where they come from and tend to see the whole thing as holiday time.' Katie worked at a summer school on the south coast and found that discipline can be a problem. 'The students' English is quite low level and they want to speak their own language all the time. Sometimes they've had enough and they're uncooperative and don't listen to you, so it's about finding a happy medium between having a rapport with them and maintaining your authority.' Melanie said she finds that, 'Discipline frightens people a lot, but is often only a major problem when the work is boring or not at the right level.' If you already worked with children before moving into ELT, you will probably agree with Neena's advice to, 'Go in tough and you can relax and soften up later when they know you.' She feels that, 'Younger students are more hyper, but more responsive as well and it really works if you reward them and make it as fun as possible, so they don't even realize they're learning.' John's advice is to, 'Have lots of games up your sleeve and use any activity programme as bribery.'

It is hard work at a summer school, but the atmosphere is usually very relaxed and informal. Teachers at Tony's school teach in the morning and are on duty in either the afternoon or the evening, but he says, 'You can't quantify the hours, so teachers can't be clock-watchers as it doesn't work like that.' Laurence, who was a qualified secondary school teacher, says, 'You always had to be on duty really and look after them, but it was different to working in school because the children were also on holiday and we did lots of games and activities and outings in the afternoon.' The staff live in as well and Neena, who took a job at a residential summer school as her first ELT job, remembers that, 'Sometimes the children were homesick or got up in the night and had midnight feasts and we spent seven weeks chasing after them at three in the morning, which was quite entertaining.' It is hard work, but Laurence says that, 'They did learn some English, which was what their parents had paid for. If it was well organized, it was good fun for you and them.'

John, who has an ELT diploma, organized summer schools where the children came to England for two weeks and lived with British families who had children of the same age. He negotiated with local schools so that the children attended school for the last week of term when the atmosphere was more relaxed and they made friends and got lots of opportunities to practise their English. In the second week, he taught English in the mornings and organized outings and social activities like ice-skating and swimming in the afternoons, evenings and weekends. Both the language learners and the British children joined in and parents sometimes helped supervise the activities. He also employed someone part-time to help and a job like this would be a good way to find out if you would enjoy teaching young learners.

Saturday schools

There are not many opportunities to teach ELT at Saturday schools in Britain but, if working with children outside the holiday period is something you enjoy, then it is worth finding out is if there is a school near where you live. Classes may be held in the school the children attend during the week or in rooms in state schools or adult education centres that have been rented for the day, so facilities will vary. Children could be anything from 4- to 12-years-old and will probably be grouped according to age rather than level, although this depends on the school.

The atmosphere at a Saturday school is more like an ordinary school than a summer school as the students are not on holiday and have been sent by their parents to learn. Rachel already had an ELT diploma when she got a job teaching Japanese children at a Saturday school. Their parents were working in Britain from anything from six months to a number of years and the children attended a Japanese school during the week, but were sent to extra English classes at the weekend. There were few discipline problems as, 'Culturally, they were used to going to school on Saturday as that's what happens in Japan and they were much more disciplined than English children would be.' Making the transition from working with adults to teaching young children can be quite difficult at first and Rachel says, 'I felt a bit out of my depth because I hadn't really got that kind of experience with children.' If you have children of your own or if you have worked with children coaching football or teaching something like swimming, then teaching at a Saturday school could be a good way of putting your experience to good use.

Private lessons

There are limited opportunities to teach private lessons to children in Britain as most young learners are on organized courses and only here during the holiday periods. There are large numbers of foreign workers in Britain, however, and some may be here long enough to bring their families and want extra lessons in the evening for their children who are at school during the day. Gladys, who had taught GCSE English to native speakers, got into ELT by accident as a parent answered her advertisement in the local paper and she agreed to take on a French child whose family was in England for a year. She had never done it before and says, 'I spoke a little French, which helped, but we got on well and I helped him with the English he needed to succeed at school. His mother used to bring him to my house and we'd look at the work he'd been doing or homework he had to do.'

Children learn very quickly, which is very rewarding, but you will also have to work hard to plan lessons that will keep them occupied. Rachel gave private lessons to children as young as four and says she found that, 'The little ones were particularly difficult and I used to find myself going into children's bookshops looking for ideas I could adapt. Financially, it probably wasn't worth it as I spent so much time on preparation.' Finding ideas may not be a problem for you if you have worked as a classroom assistant or helped out with children's clubs like the Brownies or the Woodcraft Folk as you can easily adapt activities and use them for language teaching. Like Sophie, you might have worked as an au pair and be able to use this experience to help you make the lessons useful, but fun for the children. She taught two little boys of six and seven and says, 'I loved it. The children were sweet and I used lots of games and stories to teach them English. We'd act out stories and make up songs and it was brilliant to see their English improve really quickly.' If you want to teach children privately, then a good source of ideas for activities is children's television as you will become familiar with the kind of things children enjoy and find funny and you can use the ideas in your English lessons. (For more advice on private tutoring see Chapter 3.)

3 Teaching abroad

You may want to teach abroad for a variety of reasons, but many people become interested in ELT as a way of enabling them to live and work in a particular place. Michael, who has been teaching ELT for 25 years, was interested in the Middle East and its history and wanted to find out more about the culture and people by living there and Aiden, who now teaches ESOL, had been to South and Central America as part of his degree and got into ELT because he 'wanted to find a way to fund going there again'. Alternatively, you may want a way of earning money while travelling. Adrian, who now lives and works in Spain, got into teaching as, 'A means to an end. ELT still seems to be the best way of supporting yourself abroad,' and Simon, who worked in primary schools in Britain before teaching English in South America and Spain, wanted to take some time off to do some travelling and decided ELT would be 'a good way to earn money and see the world as well'. For Patrick, who worked in Italy, Russia and Iran, ELT was 'a good chance to do something different after university', while for James, who ended up teaching abroad for 10 years, it was a case of 'leave university, don't know what to do, want to travel, let's go'.

You may already be travelling or living abroad and get into ELT by chance. Andrew was living in Israel and started in ELT, 'kind of by accident. I didn't quite know what to do in terms of a job and it was something I drifted into through private lessons.' Gary, who had trained as a secondary school teacher, was travelling in southern India and met some Australians who said, 'You're an English teacher so come and teach English in our school.' He did, and ended up being Assistant Director of Studies there. Pam was in Germany continuing her training as an opera singer and had to earn a living somehow, so she started teaching English to private students to fund her studies while Josephine went to Spain for a year and got into ELT because a friend was doing it. Whatever your motivation, there are plenty of opportunities available for you to see a lot of the world, to meet some interesting people and to finance the experience.

Whatever your situation and your motivation, it is important to be clear that you have to work in order to live abroad. John lived and taught in the Canaries for a year, but stresses that, 'If you're working abroad you're not going on holiday.' Paul, who works in ELT recruitment, points out that, 'A lot of teachers go abroad to experience travelling and living abroad and it's a bit of a shock to find out that 10 hours of your life each day is taken up by work and it always will be. You can think that you're going to be lounging about wherever it is that you want to go, but a big chunk of your day will be working.' You may be looking to travel and have a good time but Colin, who also works in recruitment, points out that employers can be very demanding. They probably want, 'an all-singing, all-dancing teacher who's adaptable and can teach learners as young as three and, within five minutes, change the classroom round and be ready to teach a businessman of 50'. You have to convince an employer that you are prepared to work in order to achieve your ambition to live somewhere abroad.

The quality of language schools varies enormously and in some places you can get work without an ELT qualification just because you speak English. James taught abroad for 10 years before doing an ELT qualification and says, 'It's about being in the right place at the right time. Certainly it's still possible in far East Asia, parts of South America and in Eastern Europe to just turn up and get work because you're British.' Patrick, who now does teacher training, agrees that in some parts of the world, 'They're crying out for people. You can just turn up as they desperately need to learn English,' but he points out that, 'It's much better to have a teaching qualification if you want to get a decent job.' (See Chapters 5 and 6.)

The education system in each country will be different and working and living conditions will vary enormously from school to school depending on the culture. If there is a particular country or part of the world that you want to live and work in, you should try to find out as much as possible about the place from somebody who has been there and get as much advice from them as possible. The thing that most helped Ricky when she went to China was that she, 'spoke to someone who had worked there and was going back'. It is also worth consulting *Teaching English Abroad* by Susan

Griffith (Vacation Work 2001), which gives information on over 100 countries.

Volunteering

Teaching as a volunteer is an excellent way to share your skills and experience and it gives you the opportunity to develop new skills and ideas that you can use in your career afterwards. Voluntary Service Overseas (VSO) is probably the best-known way of working and sharing your experience, but is a serious commitment as you usually go for at least two years. VSO is looking for qualified and or experienced teachers, so it is something to consider when you have decided that ELT is right for you. People who have worked for VSO usually find it a life-enhancing experience and most would strongly recommend it as a way of doing something worthwhile and learning about another culture (see below and Chapter 7 to find out more). If you want to try living and working abroad and want to get some ELT experience while doing something enjoyable and worthwhile, there are other ways of volunteering your skills and you could teach abroad in the summer holidays or during the gap year before going to university.

Gap year

If you have just finished your A levels and are planning to go to university, you may decide to take a gap year and do something different and exciting before studying again. There are all sorts of things you can do, but one option is to work as a volunteer English teacher somewhere that needs you. You may never teach English again, but it is possible you may get the taste for ELT and decide to take it up as a career after university. Either way, it is a marvellous chance to:

▌ live somewhere different;

▌ travel somewhere interesting;

▌ develop some new skills;

▌ find out if you enjoy ELT;

▌ do something useful and rewarding.

There are various ways you can organize your gap year and you will need to spend at least half the year raising the money to go either by working or raising sponsorship to cover your air fare, your training fees and anything other than basic survival costs. You might decide to arrange the year through 'GAP', which coordinates a variety of volunteer projects including ELT opportunities. It trains 7–8,000 young volunteers a year and sends people to 31 countries all over the world from Fiji in the South Pacific to places like Hungary and Slovakia in Eastern Europe. If you are selected as a volunteer, you will attend a one-week introductory course in Britain, which prepares you to work in primary or secondary schools. When you get to the school where you are going to work, it will provide free accommodation but Alan, who coordinates and runs the ELT introductory courses, warns that, 'You'll get free accommodation, but it could be a bit primitive. It might be a hut on sticks.' That's part of the adventure, of course, and, 'You'll also get food and a little bit of pocket money.'

Most volunteers go as teachers in their own right or as classroom assistants. Students abroad are often taught plenty of grammar in school, but are not given many opportunities to talk, so your brief would be to help the students speak English. Alan says the course is very intensive, but it is about, 'helping people learn some of the basic techniques of what to do in a classroom when they walk in on their first day'. As you will have just finished school yourself before doing your gap year, you might find it uncomfortable to be in the role of teacher, but the course gives you, 'the confidence to be in front of a group of people, managing them and telling them what to do'. Alan says that this confidence about being in the role of a teacher is very important as many volunteers will go into, 'quite traditional educational situations where the teacher is expected to be a very strong authority figure and has to be the boss who is very much respected. If you try to be too friendly, then the learners can get very confused as the roles aren't defined enough and then that's when you'll lose respect by trying to be too "pally" and too "Western" in your approach.'

The course is very practical and 'hands on' so you get some demonstration, but you spend most of the time practising different ELT techniques on your fellow trainees and trying out ways of introducing language using context. The course does not deal with grammar, so do not worry if you feel you did not do much of that at school. The focus is on ways of setting up oral work without speaking the language of the people you are teaching and making sure you have the techniques and body language to manage a group of children in a classroom. If you decide you would like to do ELT in your gap year, then you have to attend a selection interview and convince the interviewers that you can not only raise the money, but that you have the qualities and attitude needed to get the most out of the experience.

You can indicate the countries you would like to work in, but the organization will match your personality and temperament to the needs of the teaching situation. As Alan points out, 'The sort of person who's going to work in a school in a village near the base camp of Everest in Nepal is going to need different skills and different kinds of resourcefulness from someone who's going to teach refugees in Hong Kong.' You will teach for most of the time in the country you are sent to, but will also have time to travel around with other volunteers you have met there. Working in ELT in your gap year gives you a very good opportunity to have some unforgettable experiences and to explore a possible career option before going off to university.

Summer volunteering

If you are a student or have just left university and are not sure if ELT is for you, then working in a summer camp as a volunteer is a good idea. You will have the experience of living and working abroad for a month or two and will be able to see if you like working with foreign language learners. Summer camps are often for the children of middle-class parents and are usually from a week to a month long, but some are organized to provide an educational experience and holiday for less privileged children. You might be actually camping or you may live in student accommodation or dormitories with other volunteers. There are usually classes for the children in the morning and games and activities in the afternoon and evening. The children can range in age from 7 to 16 and will already have learned some English at school.

Alex worked as a volunteer at a summer school in Poland while she was at university to get some experience before she went to teach French for a year as part of her degree. It was a voluntary scheme and most of the helpers were students. They were not paid but, 'were rewarded with a holiday around Poland and basic expenses were paid'. The volunteers did not teach the formal lessons, which took place in the morning, and there were Polish assistants who looked after the children's welfare, but they organized games and outings in the afternoon. Alex says, 'It was a fun month with more games than any real teaching, but it prepared me for France.' Summer volunteering could be a good way to do something useful and to have a cheap holiday, but it could also give you a taste for ELT.

Voluntary Service Overseas (VSO)

VSO sends newly qualified and experienced ELT teachers to work in the developing world for local employers. Teaching as a volunteer is an excellent way to share your skills and experience and it gives you the opportunity to develop new skills and ideas that you can use in your career afterwards. People who have worked for VSO usually find it a life-enhancing experience and most would strongly recommend it as a way of doing something worthwhile and learning about another culture. To teach with VSO you generally must be aged 23–68 and could have a degree and some ELT experience or have a degree and have just got your ELT certificate.

It is also possible that VSO may pay for your ELT certificate course if you are a language graduate. The selection process is very careful and thorough as they need to be sure you are right for the placement and the job, so it provides you with the chance to talk to volunteers who have already worked in the country before you are interviewed. If you meet its basic requirements in terms of qualifications, you then attend an assessment day to find out if you have the skills and qualities it is looking for before finding you a placement.

Contracts are usually for two years, although roughly a third of volunteers choose to stay longer than that as they find the experience so rewarding. You go out with a group of volunteers with different skills, which means you know people before you arrive and can support each other. You also get very good support from VSO, which provides:

▌ an induction to prepare you for life in the country you will be working in;

▌ classes in the local language when you arrive;

▤ an orientation and cultural awareness course to help you find your way around the system and settle in;

▤ clean basic accommodation;

▤ a local salary;

▤ return air fares;

▤ medical insurance;

▤ pension contributions or ISA (Individual Savings Account);

▤ support when you come back to Britain.

VSO is very experienced in placing teachers abroad and produces excellent supporting information, which explains how the application and selection process works, so if you think VSO teaching could be right for you, then you can find out more by:

▤ talking on the phone to former volunteers with a similar background to yours about their experience of living and teaching abroad;

▤ looking at the Web site, which includes practical information as well as some of the personal experiences of volunteers;

▤ sending away for an information pack, which includes an application form as well as details of what VSO is looking for on the assessment day.

Private tutoring

If you travel abroad, your first introduction to English Language Teaching may well be meeting people in a café or bar, becoming friends and then being asked to teach them English. This will probably be very informal and you may ask them to teach you some of their language in exchange, but it could be a good way into some paid private tuition. If you persevere with your new friends and do try to teach them something, they may well know people or have friends who would like to employ a private tutor for lessons or English conversation. James got his first private students in Venezuela because he had friends who were doing ELT there, Andrew got his first students by, 'putting up little notices on trees with my telephone number', and Pam, 'put up ads in schools and local youth clubs'.

You may also see advertisements for private tutors and may be interested in trying this as a way into ELT. Simon put an advertisement in the local English newspaper in Madrid and says that, 'One of my first students was the wife of a diplomat. They had a grand, palatial house and I used to go there to teach and the maid would bring in wonderful sweets and biscuits.' Private tutoring can be very hard work, though, as there is usually only you and the student and conversation can be very difficult when your student has very little English or if you find you have little in common. James remembers that some of his private students were 'affluent ladies who had nothing better to do in the afternoon than chit-chat and show off their designer clothes, so it was difficult to find things to talk about'. As Pam points out, though, the lovely thing is that you are independent, 'I have nobody telling me what to do. I'm my own boss and I can decide who I want to teach.'

It can be unreliable as a source of regular income. Your students can stop classes at any time as you have no formal contract, so it is worth thinking carefully before you enthusiastically agree to an arrangement you may regret. Pam, who teaches children as well as business students, says that, 'The business people especially are liable to ring up and say they've got to go somewhere urgently and can't attend a lesson. If it happens too often then I've been known to say I can't continue teaching them.' It can be difficult as you never know how much money you will earn each month and, 'In the summer a lot of teaching is cancelled because of holidays, so it means planning ahead and making sure you've got summer intensive courses organized to fill the gaps.'

In general, though, the advantage of private teaching is that it is flexible because you can take on as many or as few students as you can get and you can arrange the times of the lessons to suit you. For Pam, who has a son, 'It means that I can plan my teaching around my family life. In Germany, children come home at lunchtime, so in the afternoon I teach at home.' In addition, as Simon says, 'Private teaching is better paid than teaching in a school or college as you cut out the middleman, so I got paid three times as much as I got paid at the school.' Private teaching will suit you if you are what Pam calls a 'self-starter'. 'No-one will do your work for you. If you don't work, you don't earn any money. Sometimes you'd rather have a day off because you're feeling a bit rough, but you can't because you won't get paid.'

Ideally, perhaps you would work some hours at a school to give you a regular income and supplement this by teaching private students. If you teach in a school, you may see notices in the school asking for extra private tuition or some of your students may ask you for private lessons. You will then need to think about the questions already raised and will also need to check that the school will allow you to take on private work. Many schools are happy for tutors to do this, but others want any arrangement and payment to go through the school, so remember to check this or you could be in trouble.

Factors to consider

You need to be sensible about this and to think about the following:

▌ What is the going hourly rate for private teaching?

▌ How many hours do you need to teach to get enough to live on or to supplement your income?

▌ Are you prepared to work in the evenings or at the weekend?

▌ Are you prepared to have students come to your home with the loss of privacy that this involves?

▌ Will you charge them for your time if they are late?

▌ Are you prepared to go to the student's home?

▌ Will you charge for your travel time?

▌ Do you feel comfortable asking the student to pay in advance for an agreed number of lessons?

▌ Will the student have to pay if they cancel?

▌ Do you feel comfortable (and is it culturally acceptable?) for you to be alone with the student if they are of the opposite sex?

Boundaries

Private tutoring can be a very good way of not only getting some experience, but of getting to know people. The boundaries between tutor/friend can be blurred (and you may be happy with this) and there is usually some hospitality involved in being in someone's home or they in yours. If you want to teach in your home, you need to have a suitable room. Pam has a blackboard, video recorder, TV and cassette recorder in her teaching room, but Jane lived in a shared flat and used to try to teach in the kitchen when she thought her flatmates would be out. 'It didn't work, though, and people were always coming in and out making coffee, so it was very disruptive and my students and flatmates got fed up with it.'

You do not want to be exploited, so you may initially need to be quite businesslike about start and finish times or you could end up being paid for an hour, but spending another drinking tea/coffee and talking English. Pam bills her students once a month and they can cancel up to 24 hours before a session, but she warns that, 'It's important to make it clear at the start that lessons should take place regularly and cancellations are an exception.' If this arrangement suits you then it is fine, but it is much easier to start by sticking to time boundaries and role boundaries and to relax these if and when you feel comfortable doing so.

In-company language teaching

Some big companies employ English teachers directly themselves and this can be excellent as both the pay and facilities are usually good. Pam works for a number of firms and says, 'They all have good teaching facilities, well-equipped with audio-visual aids, flip-charts and overhead projector.' Facilities depend on the size of the firm, of course, and 'Sometimes it's a problem finding a room in the smaller firms if they've got lots of visitors and sometimes you can end up in their canteen competing with the noise of workers on their breakfast break.'

Large firms often advertise in the newspaper for 'native speakers' for conversation practice and this can be a good route into ELT as, 'Often they were big bosses of firms looking for a possibility to "warm up" early in the morning before going to important negotiations.' For Pam in Germany, these warm-up sessions usually started at 7.30 am, but the advantage was that, 'They didn't involve any preparation and I just had to sit and listen. I was usually offered a cup of coffee and I'd just correct grammatical mistakes and suggest new expressions etc.'

You may be quite happy to stick with this sort of teaching, but it can also be a way into more formal teaching with groups of people from different departments and of different levels of ability. For Pam, the early morning lessons were a sort of apprenticeship and, 'Gradually the sessions got more demanding and I had to go through contracts with them confirming that they had understood the small print before they signed the multi-million dollar deals.' Pam's degree is in German, but she also found some of the English challenging too. 'Contracts tend to use fairly complicated legal terminology, so this could be pretty hard at times.' This kind of teaching can be extremely challenging and stimulating as you will be working in partnership with the company and shaping the job to suit your skills and strengths. Adrian, who works in Spain, says, 'I enjoy teaching professional groups most of all, doctors, lawyers, bankers etc. Learning English for them is just a means to an end and it's very rewarding watching people achieve their goals.'

There are lots of opportunities for in-company teaching in the Middle East, although these are usually for male teachers for cultural reasons. The pay and conditions are usually very good and working for one of the big oil companies for a couple of years is an excellent way to get some teaching experience and make a lot of money at the same time. You will need at least a certificate-level qualification, although some companies require more than this. Your students will be studying their technical subject, which might be oil or gas technology, and will probably have up to 15 hours of English per week. The English teachers base their teaching around the technical subject and liaise closely with the technical trainers to make sure that what they teach is directly relevant to the students' work and studies.

The company will sort out flights, accommodation and insurance and offer what Michael, who works on what is often called a 'bachelor contract' describes as, 'a very good deal'. He teaches 29 days and then has 27 days off. He works very hard during his month on as he teaches up to 28 hours a week, which is 'quite strenuous', but he is then flown back to Britain and can spend time with his wife and two young sons. The teaching conditions are generally good with small classes and highly motivated students.

The salary and working conditions are so good that you may decide to extend the contract and stay longer than the usual two or three years, but many people stay long enough to save some money or perhaps pay off their student loan after university and then move on. Michael has worked in the Middle East for six years with his present company and obviously likes the job, but he warns that, 'It's an odd existence and you're in a very vulnerable position as an overseas worker. You have no protection at all, which people should know.' There are advantages and disadvantages to any teaching situation and, if you want to earn a good salary and to enjoy good working conditions and a very comfortable lifestyle then a contract in the Middle East could offer you just that with the bonus of being flown home or to interesting travel destinations every four or five weeks.

Private language schools

If you want to be sure about the quality of where you work, then make sure the British Council or another recognized body has accredited the school. Recognition bodies are set up to monitor the standards of teaching and student welfare in schools. They:

▍ inspect schools regularly;

▍ look at the facilities and resources;

▍ observe the teaching;

▍ check the qualifications of the staff;

▍ monitor student welfare.

If the school is not a member of a recognized organization it may not mean that it is a bad one, but check whether your prospective employer has accredited status if you want to be sure that you and the students will be getting a fair deal. A school that has accreditation will use this on its publicity literature, so it is easy to find out and you can also get a list of accredited schools in a particular country from the British Council.

Many foreign language learners study at private language schools after work or college and you might teach either children or adults or both at a private language school. In John's first job in Spain, 'The huge range of students was a big challenge. I had heart surgeons really needing ESP, Spanish teachers of English just wanting to chat to a native, along with three little girls who burst into tears any time I spoke a word of English.' Some will study part-time, but others will be studying full-time to get English language qualifications or to improve their employment prospects. English is the language of the business world and, in Madrid, Simon found that, 'For anyone applying for a job it always states "good level of English required", so anyone who wanted to get somewhere in business or wanted to get another job needed English. A lot of companies sent people for classes, so my students were quite keen.'

Being sent to classes does not always make students want to learn and had the opposite effect on some of James's classes in South America. 'They might have been sent there by their company or they might be younger kids who've been sent there by their parents, so the motivation wasn't always that strong, which could be difficult.' In Portugal, Nathan was teaching, 'students who'd been at school all day and they'd come to me in the evening. They'd be yawning and fed up and they didn't hide it, so I had to work really hard.' The length of the course and the number of hours will vary from school to school and students' reasons for learning English will vary, so you will need to be flexible and to be able to cope with different teaching situations.

The classes are often fairly small, between 5 to 12 students perhaps, and may meet daily or two or three times a week. Class size varies from school to school, though, and in some parts of the world, you may be expected to teach very large groups. When Gary taught in southern India he had, 'classes of 50 to 100 sometimes and they were very mixed ability to the point where some of them couldn't write at all. There were all age groups and levels, but usually absolute beginners. They were free classes and there was a community bus that some Christian organization had donated, which would pick up people from the villages, but others would walk to get to the class.' Gary's teaching situation was very challenging, although he says, 'I loved it actually', but not uncommon in some parts of the world. It is unlikely, though, that you will have to cope with such large classes in most private language schools in Europe or South America.

Some language schools are privately owned by individuals and, as in any other field, there are some excellently run organizations and some very dubious ones. Phiona, who worked in Peru straight after doing an ELT certificate course, says, 'My first job was in Lima for a really dodgy operation and the owner was a mad English woman.' Other schools, like International House and the Bell Schools, are part of a chain run by international organizations, which have centres all over the world including Britain. If you work for one of the large chains, you can move around the world teaching at different schools. Many run their own training and staff development programmes and Neil, who works for a well-established chain, says that 'You'll be part of a team working together and there'll be a Director of Studies on hand to support you and seminars on things like teaching methods or new materials.' This can be a great advantage if you are looking for career development rather than just a job to make money while you live somewhere warm.

One-to-one in language schools

Some EFL schools offer one-to-one tuition and you may be asked to do this as part of your contract. Most of this kind of teaching is Business English as it is expensive and it is usually only for companies that can afford to pay for private lessons through a school. The teaching will take place at the school or at the premises of the company whose staff you are teaching and the school will pay you, so the issues mentioned in the previous section will not concern you. Simon worked for a language school in Madrid, which had a contract with the Spanish equivalent of British Telecom, and he did Business English one-to-one with employees of the company. He found this interesting, but warns, 'It's much harder work than teaching a class as you get through your material much more quickly and you're on show the whole time, which can be quite draining'.

One-to-one does not just mean turning up and chatting to the student in English. Pam says she has to, 'be prepared to learn all about different fields of work. Students often want to talk about their products, which can range from milling machines to moulds for the plastics industry. Sometimes I spend hours reading through materials about the company and its products before lessons.' Alex worked in Italy and taught one-to-one for companies that contacted the school and were offered classes of small groups or one-to-one. She agrees that 'One-to-one is more difficult as you have no break and you get through everything much more quickly than you'd expect. The pace is completely different and it's a lot tougher as the student is always looking straight at you and you can't make a mistake.' You can end up teaching some fairly high-powered business people and, when Gary worked in Spain, his school tended to use him for one-to-one with important clients like the Spanish equivalent of the Head of British Rail or a Head of Department in the Ministry of Home Affairs.

Working conditions

Private language schools often employ teachers on temporary contracts, which can be useful if you want to stay somewhere for a few months and move on. It might not be ideal if you want something more settled and Madeleine, who now works in Britain, had a contract for two weeks at a time. 'You looked at the timetable of the first day of the next month to see if you'd got work and how many hours. It was very insecure and not very motivational for me.' When Simon worked in Argentina, he was in an extremely precarious position. 'US teachers were given work permits, but English teachers weren't, so I was working illegally and getting paid on someone else's pay cheque. I was on a tourist visa and I had to leave the country every three months. There were English teachers there who'd been there for six years and every three months they'd have to go to Uruguay and back to renew their tourist visas.' Gary was in a similar situation in Spain and was not sure what his legal status was there as, 'The organization didn't want to go through the bureaucratic nightmare to legitimize my position, so for the first three months I was working illegally. I didn't want to be caught, so I'd leave the house looking like a casual tourist and put on a tie in the metro.'

If you plan to live overseas for a while, a year perhaps, then you will probably want a more long-term contract and Roger of International House advises that you should, 'Sort out what your contract means before you go. For example, find out what happens if you're taken on to teach 25 hours and they don't have enough students to put on that many classes. You need to know if they'll still pay you.' You are probably safest working for a large organization that employs a lot of staff and looks after them, but you may be lucky and find yourself in a small, friendly school at which everyone works together to make a go of it and your pay and conditions are good. You can work part-time, of course, which will give you time to enjoy the country and learn the language if you do not already speak it, but you may prefer the pay that goes with a full-time job or the flexibility of working for more than one school.

Most full-time language teachers teach between 25–30 hours a week and this may include evenings to cater for people who want to study after work or children coming to extra classes after school. Some schools may expect you to teach more hours, but this will be exhausting and will leave you no time to prepare your lessons or to mark the students' work, so beware any employer who expects this. Josephine taught 35 hours a week in her first job, which she says was, 'Crazy,' and this included classes on Saturday morning from 8 o'clock in the morning till 2 o'clock in the afternoon with a 15-minute break, which was, 'Pretty painful.' This is obviously an understatement and Phiona had a similarly impossible workload in her first job. 'We taught 40 hours a week from 7.30 am to 10.00 pm with classes spread over the whole day. We taught kids as young as four and most Saturday mornings,' but, after about six months she, 'saw sense and moved on'. Only agree to this kind of contract if you are absolutely desperate for money as you will soon burn out and the quality of your teaching will be dreadful.

Many of the big schools are very well equipped with books, additional resource materials, tapes, videos and a language laboratory and you will teach in light, carpeted classrooms or in the offices of the company for which you are working. Conditions will vary, of course, and it is generally the case that schools in developed countries will be better equipped and that schools that are part of a large chain are likely to offer better working conditions than small ones. The school where Simon worked in Madrid had, 'an incredible amount of really good material' and Patrick's school in Rome was, 'very well equipped in terms of resources'.

Gary's school in southern India, however, 'had no textbooks. There was one book that came from the period of the Raj and had things like how to address British officers and their wives, so that wasn't much use. There was also an occasion when we completely ran out of supplies, including paper, so we used sand trays to do exercises under a tree.' Although good resources are a great help and make the teacher's job much easier, they are not everything. You may find it challenging, but satisfying to work somewhere where you have to be resourceful and creative and make the most of what is available around you. Gary insists that, 'Despite the lack of resources it was a very, very rewarding experience. It led me to consider ELT as a career.'

Social programme

Private language schools may organize some sort of social programme for the students and expect the teachers to take part in some of the events. Unless it is part of your job to organize this, you will not be paid extra to do this, but it is a good way to get to know the students and the other teachers so you will probably enjoy it. When Ricky worked in Spain, her school had a busy formal and informal social programme where, 'Our students tended to be our friends and we went out with them afterwards. We'd also organize things like picnics and parties and, although the socializing often went on in Spanish, we'd try to do things like games in English.'

It is not like teaching at a school in Britain, though, as students already have a social life outside class and, depending on the clientele, have 'important jobs and homes to go to'. They do not need the school to help them make friends and meet people, so you cannot rely on this as a way of getting to know people. When Andrew worked in Israel he did not get to know his students socially as, 'They used to come after work and go straight home, so it was a very brisk turnaround.' Patrick had a similar experience in Italy as, 'Many of the younger ones lived at home and didn't really have a social life outside their families.'

Young learners

Teaching young learners is a boom area at the moment and there is an expanding market across Europe and beyond for teachers of EYL (English to Young Learners). English is now the mandatory language taught in schools in the state sector around the world and Andy, who has run EYL courses for more than 15 years, explains that, 'Most EU countries have now dropped the age for starting English to eight and there is also a big demand for native speakers in Japan and the Far East.' Katie, who taught abroad for six years says, 'If you work abroad, you will almost certainly find yourself teaching children at some stage, which is a whole different ball-game.'

It helps if you are young and energetic but, whatever your age, there are plenty of opportunities to teach young learners if you work abroad. Roger, who recruits teachers for schools all over the world, says, 'Everyone's doing it, but you need enormous energy as they're non-stop.' Colin, who taught young learners in Japan says that you not only need energy, but, 'enthusiasm and a willingness to make a fool of yourself. It's about being a fun-provider and about teaching lessons through a fun medium.' Games are one way of doing this, but he says, 'Singing and dancing are a must. You don't have to be very good at it, but you've certainly got to give it a go.' There is an enormous demand for EYL all over the world and middle-class parents arrange private lessons or send their children to classes in the evening after school.

Private lessons

Parents often pay for additional private lessons for their children either because they are struggling with English at school or because they want to help them get ahead and succeed at school. The issues raised earlier about private teaching apply here too and, in addition, if the lesson is at your home the parent may stay in the room while you teach their child and so you need to decide if you feel comfortable with that. It probably works better if you teach two children at the same time, so it is useful if the child has a brother or sister or a friend who would like to learn at the same time. You will also need to get hold of some teaching materials specially written for children and to think of plenty of varied activities and games so that the learners do not get bored. You have to make the learning as fun as possible and it helps if you can use drawings, cartoons and songs to keep the children's interest.

Teaching children can be very satisfying and Pam finds it, 'extremely rewarding to see the children who have been getting very bad marks at school gradually getting better and even excelling in some cases. Most of the children come with no confidence at all and it's great to see them actually enjoying English after a few months of extra lessons.' You might take on pupils for a few weeks, perhaps just before they do an exam, or the relationship may be long term. Pam is still in touch with one student, 'who started coming when he was 14, ended up going to university in England and is currently writing his doctorate'.

Young learners at private language schools

Many private language schools have recognized the demand for English for young learners and offer after-school classes for children and teenagers. Even if you have not worked with children, you may be asked to teach classes as part of your contract or it could be an area of ELT that you would like to develop. A good school will have plenty of resources available like games, videos, pictures and puzzles as well as coursebooks written specially for young learners, but you must also be prepared to make your own materials. When Alex taught young learners in France, she used lots of things like photos, comics, cartoons and games, which she had taken with her from England. This was very useful as, 'Many of the children I was with had never seen an English person or been to this country, so it helped to prove that the country existed and the language was worth learning.'

Paul worked in Japan for two years and most of his teaching was with children. 'About 80 or 90 per cent of the children were as young as three to five and, if they were exceptionally bright, they started at two and a half.' Class sizes were small with usually between 6 and 10 children and he says, 'You'll never get hundreds of children unless you're teaching in a private kindergarten where they have their own rules and you might have up to 40 children.' Even if class sizes are small, though, teaching EYL is very different to working with adults and you must be prepared to lose some of your inhibitions to enjoy it. Paul says, 'There's absolutely no way you can remain aloof and detached and retain your dignity at all. You close the door and you run about, hop, skip, jump, dance, be a dog and be a cat. You're in there three or four hours a day, so you have to enjoy it.'

Working with young learners can be great fun and very reward-ing, but you have an important responsibility as a teacher. Melanie, who trains EYL teachers, emphasizes that, 'Adult teaching is just teaching English, but EYL teaching is education of the whole child.' Jo, who trains teachers of young learners in Portugal, says that, 'Children are developing physically, emotionally and socially and language is integral to their whole development.' Andy, who runs residential EYL courses, points out that, 'You also have the respon-sibility of dealing with minors (supervision, welfare and so on) and that's something an EYL teacher must be constantly aware of.'

Chris, who is also an EYL trainer, points out that teachers have, 'an ethical consideration as your teaching will impinge on their future lives'. Whether you are teaching large or small groups of children, you have to be concerned for their safety, well-being and happiness as well as teaching them English. Chris runs training courses for EYL teachers and emphasizes that, 'You have to care about the children. If you don't have some kind of affective connection with them, you shouldn't be doing it for your own good and theirs. It can be quite damaging to the development of the child if you don't show them an unconditional, positive regard.'

The responsibility can be very daunting if you have no experience of working with young learners. Paul had just done his ELT certificate and was not really prepared when he first started working with young learners. 'I hated it for the first month. It was absolutely horrific because I didn't know what to do and they were all scared of me.' Things quickly got better as he gained experience and confidence and he, 'really, really got into it after a couple of months and enjoyed it. The younger the better and the bigger the class the better because you've got more scope to do things.' Melanie has been teaching EYL for a long time, but still finds that, 'Children constantly surprise us with what they know and what they can do', so the lessons are always different and interesting for both the learners and the teacher. If you are prepared to rise to the challenge and to get the most out of the experience of teaching young learners, then both you and the children have a lot to gain and you may even find that this is an area of ELT in which you decide to specialize.

Teaching young learners can be very rewarding and Rachel had her first experience of EYL in Brazil. 'I had a class of mid-intermediate 14-year-olds and I really enjoyed it. They were very enthusiastic and also very excited to have a native-speaker teacher and they wanted to know everything about British culture and music.' Jo enjoys the fact that, 'Children have loads of energy and creativity. They've got amazing imagination and they aren't afraid to experiment with language.' The lessons often focus on a topic or theme and Melanie says that, 'The focus for the children in an activity or task will be the outcome – the book they've made, the poster, or the puppet – so that the work is meaningful to them. For the teacher the focus is the language embedded in the tasks.' The real skill of the EYL teacher is being able to devise materials and activities that mean something to the children and that they enjoy, but which teach them English at the same time.

Working with young learners does not suit everyone, of course, and she says that, 'You have to love kids. Without that you're lost.' The learners may not always be highly motivated, though, as their parents will have sent them and they might not be happy about this. In Andy's experience, the main difference between teaching young learners and adult learners is that the 'young learner's attitude to learning is very different, particularly with pre-adolescents. Their needs and goals are usually more immediate and their motivation weaker.' Neena, who started working with young learners immediately after doing her ELT certificate, says, 'The students are there because their parents have sent them and a lot don't want to be there, so they don't turn up or they won't participate.' The willingness to attend extra classes is partly cultural as in Japan, for example, it is very common for parents to send their children to all sorts of classes and the children are used to spending long hours doing lots of work outside school.

If you are used to teaching adults or completely new to teaching it can be very difficult if your learners are uncooperative, do not listen to you or each other and insist on talking in their own language. Rachel taught another class of teenagers who were, 'quite difficult. I wasn't used to having to tell people to be quiet or to listen, but I had to with them, so it felt like a bit of a battle sometimes.' Neena noticed that, 'If they don't understand, they make jokes to avoid being embarrassed and it can get a bit out of hand. You have to be very firm sometimes.' Melanie advises that you need to, 'Enjoy working with them, but set clear discipline parameters at the outset and keep to them. Make sure they're not too strict, but that they're fair and realistic.' For learning to happen, Andy says that you have to be someone, 'who can motivate the students and understand their individual problems', and create the right environment. When you achieve this, the best thing about teaching young learners is, 'the enthusiasm and the speed of acquisition'.

State schools

You will need qualified teacher status (which means a BEd or a PGCE in Britain) to teach in state or international schools in most countries abroad. Andy, who taught young learners in Sweden, France, Tanzania and Togo, says, 'It's well worth investing in an EYL certificate as well.' In some parts of the world, you may be able to find a way around the system and, 'get a job in-country with no formal qualifications, but you may be exploited'. It is very important that you check that your qualification is recognized by the country in which you want to work. In many countries you have to go through their system of teacher training to be eligible to work there and in Spain, for example, teachers are like civil servants in Britain and are placed in a school once qualified. If you are already a qualified teacher and you do get a job in the state system, Andy advises that you should, 'Be prepared to stay at a post for at least two years. Don't just go into it for the travel prospects.'

Universities

University jobs abroad that are advertised in Britain require you to have a first degree and at least a diploma-level ELT qualification. They usually require an MA TESOL or a PhD and at least five years ELT experience, so university teaching is not usually a possibility until your career is well established Many universities offer one- or two-year contracts and they will interview you and fly you out if you are offered the job. In some countries, you will be employed as an assistant lecturer, which means that you will not have the same pay and conditions of service as native teachers and your employment rights will be limited.

It is possible, of course, that you already live abroad and are in the right place at the right time to pick up some ELT at your local university. Michael, who has taught at universities in Thailand and Singapore says that, 'Not having an MA has never been a problem at all.' He got a job setting up a pre-sessional programme at a university in Thailand and Madeline taught at a university in Poland without even a certificate-level qualification because she was a native speaker and they desperately needed teachers. Ricky, who worked as a 'foreign expert' on a testing project in China, says that, 'If you've got an MA then you'd go in at a certain level, but basically you just need the CELTA or the DELTA, as the level of the English you'll be teaching won't necessarily be that high.' If you want to make a career in university teaching, however, then it is best to move up the qualification ladder (see Chapter 6).

4 Moving and working abroad

Moving and working abroad is a very exciting opportunity although it can be quite frightening if you are going to a new country where you do not speak the language. Ricky, who worked in China for a year, says, 'If you can, think very carefully about where you want to go and make sure it's the right place for you. Find out about the food and the kinds of things that are important to you from someone who's been there.' It is also important to find out about the culture, so that you do not offend local customs or the religious beliefs of the country. Adrian, who travelled before settling in Spain, says, 'You'll get along just fine if you're careful not to tread on people's toes in the cultural sense. Be polite and sensitive to the traditions of the country you find yourself in.'

It is important to do some simple research first to avoid putting yourself in embarrassing situations. Roger, who has taught and trained teachers for many years, warns that, 'People make idiots of themselves through ignorance of very basic bits of information.' He tells the story of one of the International House schools in Brazil that, 'hired a teacher and two weeks later she left because she'd gone there to learn Spanish. It's incredible. She'd gone abroad to learn Spanish and she didn't even know that Brazilians don't speak Spanish.' Roger says that, 'You need to check what things are like to save any nasty shocks,' and recommends that you, 'Read about the place. Buy a little guidebook and you'll get everything you need from that. Don't be in the position of being in your first class in a new country and you don't even know who the president or prime minister is.'

It is also a good idea to make use of anyone you know, however indirectly, who lives in the country where you will be working. Ricky advises, 'If possible, have contacts, somebody's brother or somebody's friend that will help as you can be very lonely at first,' and try to talk to someone who has worked there. You may be very independent and enjoy the adventure of turning up somewhere and knowing nobody, but it is sensible to make the move as smooth as possible by finding out and sorting out as much as you can before you go.

Sorting out the paperwork

It is important to find out as much as you can about any paperwork that is necessary before you can work and live abroad. Ricky, who worked in Spain after leaving university, says that, 'It's very hard when you go to a new country. The best thing you can do is get everything organized for you and, once you've established your-self, then you can be all independent later.' Even if you feel that you want to be a free spirit, you should certainly:

▌ Check that you have a current passport and that it will not run out while you are away.

▌ Find out if you need a work permit or a visa and apply in good time.

▌ Check whether you need to take out medical insurance.

▌ Take out some form of travel and personal insurance and ring around to get the cheapest deal as prices vary.

▌ Find out whether you need any vaccinations before you enter the country and how far ahead you should have these. Your doctor should be able to tell you and will also tell you whether you have to pay for these.

▌ Find out how to keep up your National Insurance contributions while you are away (if you work for a large company, the British Council or VSO then these will be paid by your employer).

▌ Take photocopies of any of the certificates you received for any qualifications you have.

Rachel worked for very good employers when she went to Brazil and says that, 'It was quite complicated getting my certificates validated and having a medical and getting a visa, but the school organized everything and paid for the flights.' When James first went to South America he was just out of university and, 'didn't care at all about pensions and National Insurance contributions', but he now advises that, 'Any good employer abroad should sort out the paperwork.' You should carefully check all the formalities have been dealt with if you want to be sure that your position is legal and secure.

Your contract

When you are offered a job, it is tempting to accept at once and worry about the details later. Unless you are absolutely desperate for money, though, you should find out as much as possible about what the school expects of you and what they are prepared to give in return. Neil, who works for a large chain of schools that recruits teachers to work abroad, advises you to, 'Find out about the company and make sure it's one that will look after you and give you support when you get there.' Make sure you are clear about the details of the contract you are being offered and get someone else to go over it with you if you can. Patrick, who worked abroad for a number of years, advises that you should, 'Sort out the conditions of service very quickly as you can easily get ripped off and earn nothing.'

Of course, not all employers are out to exploit you and many are excellent, but if you are being offered a full-time post, your contract should tell you:

- how much you will be paid;
- how many hours you are expected to teach a week;
- how the hours are distributed, for example, you may be expected to teach in the evenings;
- how many hours you are expected to be on the premises preparing lessons, marking students' work or attending meetings or staff development;
- any duties apart from teaching that you are expected to perform, for example, organizing and or attending social outings or invigilating examinations;
- how many days paid holiday you are entitled to;

▮ how much notice has to be given on either side if you or your employer want to terminate the contract;

▮ if there is a probationary period you have to work before your contract becomes permanent.

Terms and conditions of employment vary enormously depending on the country you are in and the organization you work for. Some employers pay the cost of your flight there and back while others expect you to make your own arrangements. In Spain, Simon was on a 'renewable yearly contract, but they didn't pay flights. You got paid for Christmas and Easter, but not for the summer unless you did the summer school.' Some schools pay you a local salary, but give you a tax-free lump sum at the end of your contract and this might be a good way of saving some money. Other contracts offer you a tax-free salary and a lump sum as a bonus at the end of it or, like Ricky when she worked in China, you may be paid a local salary and get a lump sum at the end of the contract.

In other countries you have to pay local taxes and you also need to check whether your employer makes a contribution to your pension or whether you need to make your own arrangements for private pension contributions. Rachel's school had a pension fund to which teachers contributed, but she was able to cash in her contributions when she left after two years. The key thing is to read the small print to make sure you fully understand what is being offered and for how long. If you are not clear about the details, then try to sort things out before you go as you are in a much stronger position. Paul, who works for a large international organization and recruits teachers for Japan, spends the last 20 minutes of the selection interview, 'going over the contract as it's important they know what they're getting into. We then spend however much time is needed for people to ask questions.' If you have been recruited through one of the big agencies or by one of the big schools they will be very happy to clarify the details of your contract and to explain anything you do not understand, so do not be afraid to ask.

It is worth remembering that a local salary might not sound much when you work out the exchange rate in sterling, but the cost of living might be very low compared to Britain and you can enjoy a very comfortable lifestyle on what looks like a low salary. Simon found this in Madrid as the cost of living was much lower than in

Britain and he had enough money to go out and have a good time. The opposite can also be true, of course, and may be difficult to survive on a local salary. When Patrick worked in Rome, the British Council gave an allowance for accommodation but, 'It was still very expensive and the cost of living was actually very high,' and Ricky's local salary in China was, 'enough to live on frugally. If you did private lessons as well and if you changed your dollars on the black market, you could make a reasonable living.' You may not be comfortable about tapping into the black economy and Ricky says it took her, 'a while to get into all that', but it may be the only way to make your salary stretch, so talk to other teachers about how they manage.

Make sure you know whether you are paid weekly or monthly and whether you have to make a claim or whether the money is automatically paid into your account. Most employers pay you a month in arrears, but payment could be as much as six weeks or two months in arrears if you have to put in a claim for the hours you work. One of Pam's jobs in Germany is at an Adult Institute where, 'I get paid for a course of 16 lessons regardless of how many people turn up but, as I get paid at the end, it means I sometimes don't actually see any money for 4–5 months.' In Phiona's 'job from hell' in Peru, she was, 'paid late or never', so make sure you have enough money to live on for the first few weeks as you may not get paid for some time.

Accommodation

Finding somewhere to live is crucial as, even if you have friends abroad, you do not want to sleep on their sofa indefinitely and you will need to make sure that you can be contacted. Andrew, who worked in Israel, says that you should, 'Make sure you've done all your research about how to get all the things you need like post and phones.' Neil, a seasoned traveller who taught in a number of countries including Romania, also advises teachers to, 'Take a universal bath plug and a travel adapter, so you can have a bath and sort out some music wherever you are.'

Most large organizations provide accommodation or help you find somewhere. Rachel's school arranged accommodation for new teachers for the first two weeks, but she says that, 'In practice they provided somewhere for as long as it took to find something and they sent someone with you to look.' When James worked in Brazil, he was with a group of English teachers and, 'The school looked at ads for us and provided a van to take us round to look at various flats.' It will make your move abroad much smoother if you know that accommodation is provided and you do not have to worry about where you are going to live.

You should check, though, whether it is offered free as part of your contract or whether rent is automatically deducted from your earnings. In the Canaries, John got a very badly paid job in a school and, 'the following week went to live in the pantry of the school to save on accommodation costs'. In southern India, Gary got his keep and basic accommodation but no wages and in Portugal, Nathan was provided with accommodation as part of his salary. Unfortunately, 'It was terrible. There was a mattress on the floor and all the furniture was broken. One of the rooms I couldn't even use because it was so damp, but I just had to make do because it was the only accommodation they had at the school and I couldn't afford to get anything else.' Nathan's situation was very unfortunate, but it can be the case that you are promised more than actually materializes so do make sure you are clear about who pays for what and for how long.

You may be lucky like Michael who works in the Middle East on a contract that includes free accommodation and very comfortable living conditions. He works on an offshore island and says, 'We're very well looked after. There are Olympic-sized swimming pools, tennis courts and so on and the students are a very sociable bunch and good to mix with. You wouldn't get anything that good in Britain.' If the school does not provide accommodation, then you will need to organize it yourself and it is not always easy. Simon was fortunate in Madrid as accommodation was, 'easy to get and very reasonable and cheap', but Patrick warns that, 'In most major cities it's very difficult to find accommodation and you don't get an allowance. You go round the streets looking for signs on the wall saying "To Rent" and it can be very expensive.' For Ricky, 'It was an absolute nightmare. I wanted to live with Spanish people, but we had a hell of a job getting accommodation and it was really stressful.'

Make the most of any contacts or friends if you have to find your own accommodation and find out what is a reasonable rent locally. As in Britain, you will need to have enough money to put down for at least a month's deposit and, if you are renting a flat on your own rather than joining a flatshare, you usually have to agree to take it for a minimum of three months. It is also important to find out about the area. In Spain, Gary answered an advertisement in a newspaper and went to view the flat in the daytime. 'It looked a very nice area with window boxes and so forth, so I took the apartment. When I returned that night, the whole area had transformed itself into the red-light area.' If you are working at a language school, there may well be other teachers also looking for accommodation or with a room to rent, so ask around. Both Patrick and Alex shared a flat with two other English teachers and so did Gary after his adventures in the red-light district and this can work well as you will all be in the same situation.

Learning the language

Your time spent living and working abroad will be much easier and more enjoyable if you speak the language. When Nathan arrived in Portugal he found it, 'nerve-wracking that I didn't speak the language. I spent a lot of time studying coursebooks on my own as I really wanted to learn the language, but I couldn't understand a single word anyone said to me.' Patrick found that, 'Not being able to communicate with people on the street was difficult,' but he points out you will survive even if you do not speak the language as, 'You can always go down to the supermarket and buy food.' As you will know if you have been on holiday abroad, it is certainly possible to stay somewhere without speaking the language and it is reassuring to know that you will not starve to death.

Living and working abroad is not just about surviving, though, and you will probably feel more comfortable if you can have at least a basic conversation in the local language. Roger lived in Hungary and says that, 'It's worth learning a few phrases of the language if you don't speak it at all. I didn't speak a word of Hungarian and it was interesting because they don't expect you to be able to speak their language, but they're absolutely delighted if you can just say thank you. It shows that you're making an effort.' It is a courtesy to try and learn basic greetings and a few polite phrases and to use these wherever possible. People will often reply to you in English because they want to practise, but that does not mean they are not pleased that you have taken the trouble to learn a little of their language.

You may already speak the language of the country in which you are going to teach as you may have studied the language as part of your first degree and spent a year there or have lived there before deciding to become an English Language Teacher. James did Spanish for his degree so when he went to Brazil where they speak Portuguese, 'It wasn't that difficult and I could speak it reasonably in about six months.' Some large organizations provide you with an induction and basic language lessons before you go or when you arrive, but others leave you to your own devices. Adrian arrived in Spain with nothing but 'my brother's old BBC "Spanish for Beginners" course', but he now speaks the language fluently. If you are starting from scratch with the language, then make sure you buy yourself a bilingual dictionary and a basic phrase book at the very least.

If you have time before you go, it makes sense to enrol in classes if they are available in your area. Ricky went twice a week to evening classes in Cantonese before going to China for a year and says she could speak rudimentary Cantonese by the time she went. She says that she could not have survived without this introduction to a completely different language, but as a language teacher yourself you might find yourself critical of the methodology. Simon found that he, 'got a bit bored' with his Spanish classes and James went to Portuguese classes initially, but, 'The classes were so outrageously boring that I didn't last more than two or three weeks.' Teachers and classes vary, of course, and Andrew did a six-month intensive Hebrew course when he first went to Israel and agrees with Ricky that lessons were vital.

If you are serious about learning the language then you need to make yourself speak it. Madeleine studied Czech at home on her own while she was there and, 'just refused to speak English', so she became quite fluent in the end although it was hard work. Ricky looked for opportunities to practise her Cantonese even when she worked in a remote, agricultural area of China. 'I used to walk round the fields and chat to people as far as I could. It would always be a very limited conversation like, "Oh what a lovely fat baby you've got," or "What's that crop you're planting?" and then they'd tell me and I wouldn't understand.' It is worth persisting, though, as the experience of living and working abroad will be very different if you can communicate effectively and Andrew insists that, 'People respect you more if you learn the language.'

It is a good idea to attend classes if you can but, if this is not possible, at least buy a 'teach yourself' book with accompanying cassette, and practise listening and repeating some everyday phrases. You could make an arrangement to exchange lessons with someone, so you teach them some English in exchange for lessons in their language. Ricky did this with a Chinese girl before she went and Josephine did the same thing when she was in Spain. This kind of informal arrangement can work well and is a good way of making friends with people other than English language teachers. Other tips to help you learn the language are:

▌ Start by learning basic greetings and how to order food and drinks in restaurants.

▌ Use any opportunity you can to practise speaking the language.

▌ Listen to the local radio (and sing along to songs if you can).

▌ Watch the news, soaps and films on television.

▌ Buy a local newspaper and work out the story using the pictures and headlines to help you.

▌ Take your dictionary with you when you go out or write down new words you see on posters or advertising hoardings.

▌ Buy a grammar book and use it to look up patterns or constructions you do not understand or to find out how to form questions or negatives.

▌ Buy yourself a notebook and organize it alphabetically to record new words. If you buy an address book, it will already be divided into alphabetical sections and you can write down new words as you see them and look them up later at home or ask someone to explain them to you.

▌ Help yourself learn the names of everyday household objects by labelling them in the language you are trying to learn.

▌ Try to learn at least 10 new words every day and group them by topic to help you, eg learn the names of fruit, vegetables or items of clothing.

▌ Keep testing yourself.

- Practise saying the alphabet and counting out loud.

- Invest in a cassette recorder and some tapes and practise reading aloud and listening to yourself.

- Do not worry about making mistakes, but have a go anyway even if you are not sure that what you're saying is correct.

- Learn how to ask people to speak more slowly or to repeat what they have said.

- Use gesture or mime to help you get your meaning across or point at things you are trying to buy.

When you start your new job, it is quite easy to spend a lot of the time with other English teachers and you will also certainly speak English if you socialize with your students, so you may find it difficult to find opportunities to practise the language. When James was in Iran, he 'only made friends with those who spoke English, although it went against the grain of my wanting to be abroad', and Patrick had the same experience when he first went to Italy. 'I didn't learn any Italian at first as I was living with two other English teachers and we spent all our time with other British people. Then I did a course in the second year there and began to practise and learn Italian more effectively.'

Becoming romantically involved with a native speaker provides an additional motivation to learn the language, and Gary's Spanish improved enormously when he got a Spanish girlfriend as socializing with her friends and family gave him excellent opportunities to practise the language. This may not be culturally appropriate everywhere, of course, and you may not meet anyone you like. There is also the risk of heartbreak so you may be safer to concentrate on the language learning recommendations above. You may already be living abroad with your partner, in which case other romantic entanglements are definitely not to be recommended under the guise of language homework.

It is more difficult to learn the language if it uses a different script. Patrick, who only learned a few words of Farsi when he was in Iran, agrees that, 'It's very difficult to learn a language where the script is completely different as you can't read it or write it down.' You will probably not need to do much writing in the new language, but it is important to be able to listen and speak, so seize any opportunity to practise and do not be afraid to ask for help.

People will generally be pleased that you are trying to use their language and will be tolerant of your mistakes, particularly if you are prepared to laugh at yourself. You may want to practise copying and forming the new letters or symbols and try using the pictures on cans and packets of food to help you read the labels and test yourself at home with the names of everyday signs and labels. Make yourself sets of cards with the word on one side and the new word on the other and practise reading them and turning over to check in English. Looking at comics and magazines with lots of pictures should also help you to make intelligent guesses about what has been written.

If you become interested in studying the language for its own sake and beyond the level of survival, then you can continue with regular classes in addition to studying on your own. Madeleine recommends, 'Do an activity that gets you to meet the locals,' and Simon found that an excellent way of improving his Spanish was to join evening classes to learn other things in which he was interested. 'I did an art history class, an ecology class and a dance class and I joined a walking club where I was the only English person.' Obviously this will not work if you are a complete beginner, but it is a good way to create opportunities to learn and practise the language, especially if you are somewhere where there are a lot of English people. As you get better at the language, you will find that reading newspapers and novels is a good way to extend your vocabulary and to familiarize you with different ways of saying things. Ask people to explain things you do not understand and try to use new words as you find out their meanings; you can also ask friends to tell you if you are using new words correctly and tell people that you are happy if they correct you. The key thing is to speak, read and listen to the language as often as you can and to make friends with people who are not English teachers.

Settling in and making friends

Teaching abroad can be quite lonely unless you quickly settle in and make friends. Andrew found that, 'It can be quite a devastating feeling if you're on your own in a foreign country,' and Nathan says that he 'always felt homesick'. When Madeleine was in Poland she, 'was lonely at times when I wasn't in a big, young, lively school', and when James worked in South America, he certainly found that he got a little homesick for his family. Both Michael and Patrick agree that, 'You do get culture shock, it doesn't matter where you go.' If you do feel lonely or homesick at times, it is important to know that most teachers experience this at some time and that these feelings do pass. As Ricky found, once you start to meet people, it gets better and, 'The more you get out and do things, the more people you run into and the more you realize there's an awful lot out there.' Simon agrees that, 'You have to make the effort to meet people and the onus is on you to try to make friends.'

Teachers at the school where you work will probably be friendly and will be able to offer lots of good advice about where to go and what to do. Rachel was lucky in Brazil as, 'I was the only native-speaker teacher at the centre and all the rest were Brazilians, so it was easy to integrate as people were very friendly.' Some recruitment agencies and schools give you an induction into the country before you arrive and others organize support when you arrive. When Neil worked in Romania, the organization 'employed a local chap who looked after everything for us. He helped us with everything from food to finding TV channels and he was brilliant.' When Alex was in Italy she was, 'sharing a flat with two other teachers, so we could go out together and meet people.' Patrick also lived with two other teachers in Rome, but found that, 'We spoke English and spent all our time with other English people.' It is useful to have other teachers to make friends with, but Paul worked in Japan and Spain and warns that, 'You won't meet local people if you hang around with teachers all the time. It's a nice safety net to have a group of people that you can switch off with and that you don't have to speak pidgin English with, but you need to get up, go out and meet some people and talk to them.'

If you want to meet British people who are not language teachers, then find out if there is a local English language bookshop, which is often a good way of finding out about events like concerts, plays or lectures. In Sri Lanka, Keith found that the local cricket club had a monthly jazz club, which attracted a mixture of Europeans and local people who shared an interest in the music. He also joined the Columbo Amateur Dramatic Society, which was looking for people to help backstage as well as to act. They put on some very good productions and it was a way of meeting other foreigners as well as Sri Lankans. Joining a language class yourself is also a good way to meet other foreigners. If the town or city where you work has a university, you might be able to join the overseas students' club and if you are interested in sport, then you will meet people if you join a local club and make use of the sports facilities.

It is also important to be prepared to chat to anyone you meet at bus stops, at the supermarket or in cafés. This may not be something you do at home and these casual conversations are likely to remain fairly superficial, but they are a good way to practise the language and will help make you feel as though you are part of the community. In China, Ricky made a big effort to talk to everyone she could and became good friends with a family that ran a shop and Patrick found that he made some Italian friends when he stopped living with other English teachers and was more on his own. It depends where you live, of course, but Keith points out that you do need to be sensitive to possible issues about money. In Sri Lanka, he found that, 'The majority of people don't earn the same amount of money as you do, so either you're taking them out or you're mixing with some fairly high-powered types because they earn the same as you. A lot of social life revolved around the five-star hotels. We'd go for meals and drinks, which were quite cheap for us, but most local people couldn't afford them.' If you want to get to know local people socially, then you need to be aware of how your salary relates to theirs and to think about how you want to handle the difference if you earn a lot more than local teachers and your students.

Many towns and cities have bars that model themselves on British pubs or American bars and you may find 'regulars' who are happy to make friends. Adrian used to, 'go for "vinos" in the taverns of the old city', and in South America, James says he, 'tended to spend quite a lot of time in bars as they tend to be centres of social activity'. This does not suit everyone as a way of making friends and Nathan, 'didn't want to just go out drinking every night', when he was in Portugal. You may not feel comfortable sitting around in bars if you are a woman on your own and, in many places, it would not be culturally acceptable for a woman to drink alone in a bar. You may work in a country where bars are not part of the culture, for example anywhere in the Middle East and, in any case, you need to be careful as you could end up trapped with the local bore or drunk or both.

One of your reasons for being abroad is probably to live somewhere different and have new experiences, so you do not want to spend all your free time with other foreigners. When James worked in Iran he found that, 'There was a whole sort of parallel lifestyle of ex-pats and that just took over,' and Simon found in Madrid that, 'There are a lot of English teachers and a lot of the life centres on the Irish pubs.' It is often quite difficult to get to know the locals, but try and avoid the 'ex-pat syndrome' in which you spend all your free time with other British people. Colin says that, 'It's great having an ex-pat lifestyle, but to get the full benefit out of being abroad, you should involve yourself in other things, whether it's sport or other community activities.' In Poland, Phiona found the worst thing was, 'huge crowds of teachers who just want to socialize together, which gets very boring after a while', and this is particularly true if they talk about work all the time.

Colin suggests that you definitely need to follow up outside interests. His background was in plant physiology, so, 'When I went to the Czech Republic I got involved in planting trees and I chose Japan to look at Japanese gardens. Apart from teaching, I went to look at loads of different gardens and even got involved building some English gardens out there.' The strategy worked and he met lots of local people and, 'had a fantastic time abroad'. Simon, who joined evening classes at which there were mostly Spanish people, says that, 'It's important to do something like that if you go somewhere where there's lots of British people.' If you do not already have an interest that you can follow up when you are abroad, then branch out and develop an interest in something new that local people do and obviously enjoy.

You may meet people through your students and many may want to invite you for coffee or a meal. Nathan spent all his time with his students in Portugal, and in Spain Gary, 'got to know a lot of Spanish people through the students and got invited to social events'. In Madrid, Ricky made many friends and says, 'It was brilliant. People were very open and friendly and you could barely walk down the street without making friends, but a lot of my friends were through my students. Our friends tended to be our students and we went out with them afterwards.' Alex found that, 'The Italians were very friendly and the students were my age so we could socialize with them,' and Patrick also made friends through the students, 'They enjoyed making British friends and they liked the different cultural aspect.' It can also be the case, as James found, that, 'If you're teaching abroad, you're also one of the only English people they've ever seen, so you have a kind of kudos and there's an interest in you as an English person.'

If your students are always looking for ways to get extra English practice, though, you may end up feeling as though you are always working. In China, Ricky felt that, 'They were all using me to practise their English. There'd be a knock on the door and they'd say, "You do this translation for me" or they'd invite themselves round in the evening and say, "I've come to practise my English with you". It was like, "You're a teacher, so that's what you're here for".' It will probably be the case that people will want to talk to you because you are English and they will not only want to practise their own English, but will want to ask you about British culture and customs and culture. The sensible thing is to use your judgement and to be willing to help people and talk to them, but avoid getting exploited. There are bound to be plenty of things you want to know about their culture and language, so exchanging information and helping each other is a good way to make friends.

It may not always be possible to make friends through your students. They might be much younger than you and have very different interests. Sarah worked in different parts of Italy for 10 years and found that making friends with her students, 'was fine in my 20s as my students were the same age. In my 30s it was more difficult as I didn't have so much in common with them any more.' Andrew says that in Israel he, 'didn't get to know the students really as they used to come after work and go straight home'. Alex was teaching in France as part of her degree and her French was fluent, but she found it, 'very, very difficult to make proper French friends. I was in a small town and there wasn't really anything going on for anyone of my age.' Ricky thinks that, 'It depends. In some societies, people are just really friendly.'

Many people feel quite homesick after the first novelty of moving abroad has worn off and this may be worse if you are working somewhere quite isolated without many other English speakers. When Ricky worked in China she, 'got terribly lonely because I was the only European and there was nobody remotely like me', and, even if you have lived abroad before, the feeling can overwhelm you after the first couple of months. If this happens to you, do not feel that you have to pack your bags and take the first plane home. Annette, who taught in Italy and now works in ELT recruitment, says, 'It takes at least two or three months for you to settle in a place and you're not necessarily going to like it immediately. Wherever you go, you can't make brilliant friends in a week.' Talk to other teachers who will probably have felt the same thing or try including some small rituals from home, for example eating Marmite on your morning toast or listening to the World Service as you go to sleep. In China, Ricky missed English tea and found that, 'They mostly had green tea, but you could get black tea and there was this very sweet condensed milk. I used to put that in as it was the nearest thing you could get to a cup of English tea.'

These reminders of home could make you feel more homesick, of course, and it may work better for you to 'go native' and adopt as many local habits as possible, for example, drinking mint tea rather than tea with milk, which never tastes the same as it does at home. It is also important to remember why you moved abroad in the first place. Phiona worked in Peru and says, 'You're always meeting local people wherever you go and you learn so much more about a place living in it than you ever do travelling there.' James's intention was, 'to integrate and to feel part of the culture and to experience it a bit', and for Madeleine, 'The more you can take out of the culture by immersing yourself in it the better. You can really get to know people while you're living in their culture.' The important thing to remember is that feelings of homesickness do pass and by the time you have been teaching for a term you will probably feel as though you have settled in.

To get the most out of the experience of living abroad it is important to try and be positive about cultural differences and not to focus on what you cannot do or get abroad that you could at home. Michael, who has taught abroad in different countries for 25 years says, 'Enjoy it. You have to be very flexible about the whole thing.' Although Ricky tried to drink something that resembled English tea, she definitely wanted to enjoy things Chinese so she, 'always ate in the canteen, despite the fact that it was infested with rats. When you went past at night, you saw the kitchen covered with rats, but I thought, "The Chinese aren't dying" so I continued to eat there and the food was actually very good.' That sounds rather horrible, but it makes a good story later and shows a willingness to adapt to different ways of living. In Poland, Madeleine, 'loved the fact that I couldn't get baked beans and takeaways and I loved queuing for bread because it was all so different'. Enjoy the differences if you can and retain an openness and an interest in the people and, as Ricky says, 'Go to interesting places if you can and have a good time and make the most of it.'

The European University of Ireland (EUI) provides a convenient, efficient and flexible platform for those wishes to improve personal skills and self-esteem. The former Mayor of Southwark Cllr Harry (2000 to 2001) agrees that cost effective programmes similar to EUI's can be a great benefit to those on low-income bracket.

EUI programmes are modelled along the well-received American concepts towards professional development.

"Very innovative and down to earth" says Sir Niall Horan, Deputy Chairman of ICEA. The president of EUI, Dr Bernard Hephrun hopes to offer a joint Masters programme in Education with English as major, the programme will be taught over a period of 24 months. The programme will be conducted jointly with a reputable university in the far eastern region, especially to enable those could not travel abroad to a western country to improve their knowledge and skills.

The assessment will be based on Assignments, workshops and dissertation.

For further information please write by enclosing your CV to: admin@europeanuniversity-ireland.com.Or write to EUI, 41 Lower Dominic Street, Dublin 1, Republic of Ireland. Fax: + 35 31 8733612

5 Initial qualifications in ELT

If you are serious about wanting to work in ELT, then you need to get a qualification. Going on a course will give you some idea of what to do in the classroom and a recognized qualification will mean that employers are more likely to take you seriously and offer you a reasonable salary. The first qualifications in ELT were introduced in the 1970s, but there is now a proliferation of courses you can do and a variety of training routes you can take, depending on whether you want to work:

▌ with adults or children;

▌ in the state or private sector;

▌ in Britain or abroad;

▌ in EFL or ESOL or both.

Just turning up somewhere abroad and starting to teach may seem like an easy option if you want to travel and pay your way, but the fact that you can speak English does not necessarily mean you can teach it. Alex, who got an ELT certificate before working in Poland, France and Italy, says that, 'People who go abroad sometimes think that because you speak the language you have the ability to teach it, but that isn't the case at all.' When Simon worked abroad he found that, 'A number of people, who haven't got a qualification, rely totally on just bluffing their way through and being matey with the students. They don't know what to say when a student comes up and says, "What's a phrasal verb?" ' It can be a terrifying prospect to be faced with a class of adult learners who expect you to know what you are doing when, in fact, you have never taught before. It is also likely that an employer who is prepared to take on staff without any qualifications is not offering particularly good pay or conditions of employment, so be careful if you accept work of this kind.

If you want to stay in Britain, you will need at least a certificate-level qualification whether you work in the state sector or for reputable schools in the private sector and to get a full-time permanent job you generally need a diploma. You might be coming into ELT from a number of different starting positions. You may be working as a volunteer and want to progress to paid work or you may have taught abroad without a qualification, enjoyed it and now want some recognition that you know what you are doing. You might have just graduated and want to travel for a while or you may never have taught, but want to embark on a change of direction. Sooner or later, though, you will need to do a training course and the important thing is to choose one that leads to a recognized ELT qualification.

Introductory courses

Some places advertise short one-day, weekend or one-week courses, which may be useful as a 'taster' to help you find out if ELT is right for you. This kind of course is useful if you have never taught at all as they give you some idea of what is involved in ELT. You will usually get a certificate of some kind, but the courses are not long enough to give you a recognized qualification. Keith did a weekend introductory course, which was, 'billed as a passport to jobs', and, if you are going abroad to somewhere that is desperate for teachers, then it may be enough to get you work. Schools in Britain that do not have ARELS or British Council recognition may be prepared to employ you part-time in the summer when they need extra teachers, but an accredited school will be very unlikely to employ you if you have only done a taster course.

As an introduction to ELT, though, such short courses are very useful and show you sample ELT materials and give you the chance to see videos of a variety of classes. You also get the chance to experiment with basic teaching techniques to present something to the other people on the course and do some activities to develop your own knowledge of English and how it works. Keith took the course after being made redundant from his accountancy job with a big company. He bought a round-the-world ticket and did some travelling and thought, 'What am I doing with my life? I want to do more than this,' and now plans to travel again to the Far East and do some teaching. The course included advice about applying for jobs, examples of previous students who had got work and participants also got a pack, which included a useful reading list, a couple of sample lessons and some materials at different levels. Keith was, 'worried the course would be too light, but it seemed very intense and practical and had a good buzz to it'.

The advantage of an introductory course is that you can decide fairly quickly that ELT is not for you without having invested a lot of your time and money. Keith says he, 'knew nothing about ELT', and would recommend a taster course. He says, 'Suck it and see. Why not do it?' If you find you enjoy the experience of ELT, you can also use the course as a springboard into work abroad or a preparation for further training or both. Courses can cost anything from £35 for a day's course to £250 at the time of writing for a weekend and may be run by colleges or private individuals in a hotel or language school.

ESOL-specific training

Some ELT courses do not make a distinction between EFL and ESOL and prepare you to teach either, but there are some ESOL-specific courses you can do if you are sure that you want to stay in Britain. These courses will be provided by your employer or by a further education college and the quality of training is often very good. The training does not always lead to a nationally recognized qualification, which may not matter to you if you want to continue teaching in your locality and are not planning to move from job to job. Other training leads to certification from City and Guilds, which is nationally recognized, or from the Open College Network, which is beginning to gain acceptance nationally.

Some boroughs join forces to offer ESOL training to tutors or volunteers in ESOL who want to develop their classroom skills and techniques, but are not ready for the demands of a certificate-level course or are not sure if they want a full-time career in ELT. Sue teaches on a part-time course, which runs over a term and was developed by two neighbouring colleges and the local adult education service in response to, 'a drastic shortage of ESOL teachers'. She says, 'The course is seen very much as a step towards the CELTA, but it gives people time to get on with other things in their lives as well.' You can use this kind of course as a route into ELT and it is an excellent way to give you some supervised practice in the classroom and the opportunity to observe qualified, experienced teachers at work. You will also start to learn about the English language and how it is structured, which is important if you are going to teach it.

ESOL volunteer training

Adult education services and community groups in Britain use volunteers in some of their ESOL classes and for home tuition (see Chapter 1) and this can be a good introduction to ELT. You will be allocated a student to teach and be offered a volunteer training programme with an introduction before you start working with students and some ongoing input sessions once you start teaching. These might be on a Saturday morning and could be over a period of six weeks or a term.

City and Guilds Initial Certificate in Teaching ESOL

Training does not always lead to a qualification, but some boroughs offer the City and Guilds 9281 Initial Certificate in Teaching ESOL. You will be working as a volunteer tutor while doing the course and usually working with a student in a qualified teacher's class, although you might also be a home tutor teaching your student in their own house. You look at how to:

- assess your student's language needs;
- plan a lesson;
- choose resources and materials and adapt them;
- analyse language;
- use some basic teaching methods;
- assess what your student has learned.

You produce assignments based on the work you are doing and you are observed teaching your student. Volunteer training is particularly useful if you have never taught and, if you get the City and Guilds 9281, you can feel that you have received some recognition of what you can do. An initial qualification also signals that you are serious about wanting to work in ELT and is often used as a route into further training and teaching.

Certificate in Teaching ESOL

If you know you want to stay in Britain and work in ESOL, you may progress to teaching groups of learners and many boroughs offer the City and Guilds 9285 Certificate in Teaching ESOL to Adults. This is a course you do while you are teaching, so is not something you can go and do intensively. It might be offered part-time over a year and you attend classes as well as continuing to teach your own ESOL students. You will learn more about the topics you studied on your initial certificate, but examine them in more depth and will also look at how:

- people learn a second language;
- to develop your students' literacy skills;
- to use ICT to support your students' learning;
- to manage groups of learners with different needs;
- to use aids and resources effectively;
- to give your student advice and guidance about progression.

You will be assessed on the teaching you do and will be observed not only in the classroom, but doing a variety of other activities with students like initial assessment of their language needs or offering support and guidance. You will also collect a portfolio of evidence to demonstrate that you are a competent teacher. This will include things like:

- course programmes you have devised;
- lesson plans;
- examples of teaching materials you have made or adapted;
- examples of feedback and advice you have given your students.

You have to show that you can meet a large number of specific competencies to pass the course. As on any NVQ course, you are assessed using a mixture of observation on the job and the collection of evidence.

This could suit you well as you collect evidence of what you are actually doing on the job. Jane, who started the 9285 certificate when she began working with a group of learners, liked the fact that, 'I could use everything I did as evidence of competence, so nothing was wasted,' but some people find it very frustrating to be asked to produce paper documentation of everything they do. Fiona, an experienced teacher when she did her 9285, says, 'It drove me mad and I couldn't get my head around all the little itty-bitty competencies.' Susan was also an experienced teacher and says, 'I'd much rather do a traditional course with proper assignments than collect bits of paper for a portfolio of evidence.' The qualification could be ideal for you, though, if you like to take things slowly and are very organized and methodical. It gives you the chance to demonstrate all the different skills you have and you are not put under the pressure of assignment deadlines and exams.

Distance learning certificates

Some certificate courses are offered via distance learning, which means that you do not attend a college and meet other trainees, but you study at home in your own time. You are sent reading tasks and assignments, which are marked and sent back with detailed feedback. This may be convenient if you are not free to attend a course full- or part-time or if you live abroad somewhere where ELT courses are not offered locally. If you really want to learn how to teach, you should make sure that the course includes a strong element of teaching practice. You should get the opportunity to be observed teaching classes and receive detailed feedback as you need the chance to put the theory into practice with actual language learners. It is important to check that the course leads to a recognized qualification or you could be wasting your time and money. BATQI (the British Association of TESOL Qualifying Institutions) publishes a register of accredited courses, so it is worth consulting it before paying for a course.

UCLES and Trinity certificates in ELT

The two best-known certificates are the UCLES CELTA (the University of Cambridge Language Examinations Syndicate Certificate in English Language Teaching to Adults) and the Trinity Certificate in English Language Teaching. When you are ready to start looking for jobs, you will see that these are what most employers ask for as a minimum both in Britain and abroad. The UCLES course has been around longer than the Trinity and old-established centres that have been doing teacher training for many years tend to offer this. The Trinity certificate is newer, but is equally well thought of and the differences between the two courses are small. On the CELTA, for example, you get more opportunity to observe experienced teachers as part of the course, but on the Trinity you study a foreign language. Martin, who works for a well established chain of private language schools that offers both UCLES and Trinity courses at different centres, says, 'Essentially they're equivalent as they're both internationally recognized, but my advice is to look at the centre itself and see what it has to offer. What's on offer at the centre is what's most important for trainees.' You usually attend full-time for four or five weeks or part-time over a couple of terms.

Teachers who have done a certificate course usually recommend it highly. Andrew did a certificate after being an estate agent for seven years and would, 'recommend it to people even if they don't want to teach. It was a huge learning curve, but when it clicked it was quite a revelation as I suddenly realized what I was doing and why I was doing it.' Andrea, who had taught ELT before she did her certificate, says, 'In order to do ELT well, you absolutely need to go on a course,' and Liz, who was on the same course, says, 'I'd certainly recommend it and my only regret is that I didn't do it earlier.'

Certificate courses are extremely practical and Alan, who now trains teachers himself, says, 'It was such an incredibly different experience to anything I'd done. I'd spent four years doing a BEd and came out a qualified teacher, but in four weeks of the certificate I learnt more about what to do in the classroom than I did in four years.' Gary, who had taught in India and was also a qualified secondary school teacher when he took his certificate says, 'It was like lighting the first candle in a darkened room. It was that first candle for me.'

You can take a course in Britain at an FE college, private language schools or university, but certificate courses are also offered abroad in countries like Spain, Poland, Egypt and Turkey and some centres guarantee a job if you pass with a good enough grade. Paul did his certificate in Cairo as he, 'fancied doing something a little bit different', and, 'loved it as it was all new and exciting'. Sean did his certificate in Madrid, as a friend who lived there suggested it and he wanted to travel. Accommodation was included in the price and, as the cost of living in Spain is cheaper than in Britain, he reckons that it was cheaper for him to spend a month doing the course in Spain than in London. He was, 'surprised that it was very hard work', but he already spoke Spanish and, 'definitely had a good time there although I did coursework most weekends'. If you are doing an ELT course because you know you want to travel, then doing it abroad is a good start and many centres offer you a job at one of their schools abroad if you are successful.

The trainees

There is usually a wide range of people with different backgrounds on an ELT certificate course. It used to be the case that the majority of people on an intensive course would be recent graduates wanting to go abroad, but that has certainly changed. There will be people in their 20s who are just beginning their ELT careers as well as people in their 50s who are starting a second or third career. Martin, who trains teachers at a private language school, says that the average age of students on his courses is mid-30s, but he usually has three or four over 55. Liz, did the certificate when she was in her early 60s and says, 'I was the oldest on the course, but I didn't find that a problem at all. We all got on really well and I'm only sorry I didn't do the course when I was younger and in my 50s.' Roger, who has trained teachers for many years, recently had a man of 74 on one of his courses, so it is never too late to retrain and take an ELT certificate course.

It also used to be the case that students on the course had to be native speakers of English as there were other training routes for overseas teachers of English or for ESOL teachers, many of whom are bilingual. You no longer have to be a native speaker to do an ELT certificate, so trainees on the course may speak a variety of languages and come from anywhere in the world. On the last two courses, James has had trainees from Italy, Greece, Turkey and

Pakistan as well as Canada and Britain. If you are not a native speaker, then your English needs to be good enough for your students to have confidence in your ability to teach it, which usually means that you:

▌ have a qualification like the Cambridge Proficiency in English;

▌ have studied English at university in your own country;

▌ have lived in Britain for a long time and become very fluent in the language;

▌ are bilingual and speak English as well as you speak your first language.

Entry requirements

UCLES and Trinity, which award the qualifications, set the minimum entry requirements, but centres will have their own selection procedures. Generally, you should:

▌ Be at least 20 years old.

▌ Be a fluent speaker of English and your spoken and written language should be free of serious mistakes or errors. This means you should be a native speaker of English or have near-nativelike ability in English.

▌ Have qualifications that would allow you to progress to higher education in your country. In Britain, for example, you should have at least A levels, a GNVQ Advanced Certificate or a BTEC National Certificate.

▌ Have an awareness of language and how it works. Entry to certificate courses is usually by interview and you can also expect to be asked to do a piece of writing and some language awareness activities to see how much grammar you already know and whether you have a 'feel' for language.

The Trinity course also requires that you have studied and can speak a foreign language. In exceptional circumstances you may get a place on a certificate course without qualifications at degree-entry level. For example, you may have worked for a number of years or have vocational qualifications, but this is unusual and you should check the entry requirements of the course you want to do. If you left school at 16 and have not studied since, you would probably not get a place on a certificate course and would find the level and amount of work difficult.

Although a number of institutions have devised their own certificate-level courses and offer their own accreditation, it is best to get a qualification that is nationally and internationally recognized, as this gives you a passport to work in Britain or abroad. If you want to find a place near you that offers UCLES or Trinity courses, you can get a list of centres from the examination boards themselves and centres will also make it clear in their publicity whether the course on offer is one of these two.

Course content

Certificate courses are what is known as pre-service, which means they assume you have not taught ELT before and that you are starting from the basics. They include a mixture of theory and practice, so you have some taught sessions and some sessions where you are teaching yourself and learning by doing. Alan says his course gave him, 'the background and framework for presenting language and some of the methodology and it did help a lot. Otherwise, you really would have no idea of what to do.'

You will look at some of the basics about how English works, which includes finding out more about grammar and phonology, which is the sound system of the language. You will be asked to buy a grammar book and will develop your own knowledge of English grammar as well as looking at how to teach it. Andrew says that, 'Before the course, I didn't really know how to teach. The course taught me about structuring a lesson and basically about grammar. I didn't know what a verb was before I did the course.' Liz says, 'I hadn't thought about the grammar of English for 40-odd years, so I realized I'd have to do a bit of work, but I enjoyed going into the language in a bit more detail.' If you have learnt another language and can speak it well, you will be already be familiar with some grammatical terms. If grammar is new to you, the course will teach you the rudiments of how to analyse and describe your own language. Alex found the course valuable as, 'It enabled me to look at English as a structured language, breaking it down and giving me different ways to approach teaching it and putting it in context.'

There will also be practical sessions about how to teach, where you will learn different methods and techniques to present and practise spoken and written language. You will learn how to plan lessons and how to use a variety of aids like the whiteboard, pictures and the tape-recorder. You will have the opportunity to familiarize yourself with some published ELT materials and also to adapt and make your own teaching materials to use with classes. As part of the course, you will usually have the opportunity to watch a number of experienced teachers actually teaching, which is a very good way of learning. Andrea found that, 'the opportunity to watch other people teach is invaluable because you benefit from their experience and learn some really good tricks.'

There will not be a lot of theory on an introductory course, but you will look at how people learn languages and, on the Trinity course, you will learn a foreign language and keep a journal about the experience. You will also look at the rationale behind the ELT methodology commonly used. Rodney, who did the course in his 50s, was surprised by the concept that, 'The teacher should speak as little as possible to enable the student maximum opportunity to use English.' The tutors will use many of the teaching methods they expect you to use with your students so you will not have many lectures, but will do plenty of discovery activities in pairs or small groups and be encouraged to work together to notice and discover things for yourself. You will also be given a reading list and be expected to do a lot of work on your own at home. Andrea says that the course is perfectly manageable as long as you don't, 'go mad and smoke 20 fags a day and stay up all night in order to shine. Do what you need to do to pass and you'll get through. You can learn a lot without totally exhausting yourself.'

An important part of the course is teaching practice, which is where you teach real language students and try out the ideas suggested on the course. There will be classes for you to practise on and you will start teaching within the first few days of an intensive course. On Rodney's course, 'There was a gradual build-up of teaching practice culminating in taking a "real class".' You will generally start by doing a short teaching slot, perhaps 20 minutes, and this will gradually increase so that you are able to plan and teach an hour's lesson by the end of the course. For Steve, 'The great strength of a course like this is that you're teaching from day one. We did 10 minutes on the first day. It was nerve-wracking, but I enjoyed it as it dealt with the fear issue at once. It was, 'Welcome, and this afternoon you're teaching. . .' There is no need to worry, though, as you will be given plenty of support both from the tutors and your colleagues on the course and Steve found that, 'There was a very supportive, affirming atmosphere.'

You will be observed by a tutor and other students on your course and will get detailed feedback on how you have performed. This can be difficult and Simon says that, 'You have to be quite robust as it's a rough kind of criticism that you get,' but students on certificate courses usually say that they learn most from this practical experience and you develop very close and supportive relationships with your fellow trainees. Gary says that, 'It was teacher-trainers pointing out obvious things that I just hadn't considered that helped me the most I think.' You will be expected to teach students at different levels and try out different techniques and you will also become familiar with some useful classroom materials.

Assessment

Certificate courses are not assessed by an exam, but you will do written assignments during the course and will also be assessed on your practical teaching. Liz, who had not studied for a long time before doing the course, says, 'I was a bit apprehensive about the assignments as I hadn't done any for a long time, but I liked using my brain again.' Your results are graded and you can get an A, B, or C grade pass or you may be graded Distinction, Pass or Fail. However your course is assessed or graded, though, you will be given plenty of feedback on how you are doing and very clear guidelines about what you have to do to be successful. As with any qualification worth having, merely attending does not mean you automatically pass and Liz says, 'It was quite taxing and it was a real challenge to do it so I was delighted when I succeeded.' Some people do fail, unfortunately, so you should be prepared to work very hard in order to get your certificate, which could be your passport to a new career.

Costs

You can expect to pay anything between £650 and £1,500 at the time of writing for a certificate course, so it is a significant invest-ment particularly if you study full-time and cannot work for a month. If you do the course intensively at a private language school, accommodation may be provided at an extra cost. Fees at state colleges are generally lower than in private language schools and you may be able to get a concession on your tuition fees if you are not working and receiving state benefits. Courses start at different times and have different fees, so it is worth shopping around to find a course that is at the right price and at the right time to meet your needs. You should also be prepared to buy some books and need to include travel costs when you are working out your budget. The courses do not attract government or local authority grants, but if you study in Britain you may be able to use your ILA (Individual Learning Account) towards the fees.

Intensive courses

Many certificate courses are intensive, which means you attend full-time for four or five weeks. This can work extremely well if you can afford to study full-time without an income and have few outside commitments like family or children. Rodney, who did the course in his 50s, found it, 'a revelation. I would recommend an intensive course because it has a momentum that I think a longer course might lack.' The advantage is that you can get your qualification quickly and start looking for paid work at once and you can also concentrate almost exclusively on the course and put everything into practice at once while it is still fresh. Cristine, who is French and did her course in England, says, 'It's good for people who want to travel and earn some money, because it's very quick. It was hard and there was a lot of work, but the advantage was that it only lasts four weeks so you can put your energy into it.' Simon says that, 'It's difficult to assimilate everything on an intensive course, but I thought it was a very good course,' but Alex, who did the course before going to teach in France as part of her degree, warns that, 'It was very tough. We were warned at the beginning that it would be tough, but I don't think any of us were expecting it to be quite that hard.'

You will probably develop very close, supportive relationships with other trainees on your course and will teach together in groups of three or four. Simon welcomed the fact that, 'You get a lot of intensive practice with a small group of peers,' and Madeleine also liked, 'the fact that you're seeing the same people every day.' Alex says that, 'We worked well together and there was always support around,' but you have to be prepared to work in the evenings outside course hours and probably meet up with your colleagues to plan lessons or to work on assignments.

The downside of doing an intensive course is that it does not leave you much time for the rest of your life, and for Alex, 'You were working all the time and you didn't stop thinking about it.' Nathan agrees that, 'It was the most difficult course of my life, it was much harder than my degree. The level was the same, but you were working all the time and you didn't stop thinking about it. I was up till 3.00 am in the morning most nights preparing lessons and finishing off assignments, but it was so good and I had such a good time on it.' You should be someone who works well under pressure to get the most out of it and intensive courses are ideal if you are someone who likes to get on with things quickly. Madeleine found it, 'good to just concentrate on one thing. It was relief really.' If you want to start your new career at once you could start your first ELT job the week after finishing the course.

Part-time courses

Part-time courses are generally two evenings or an afternoon and evening a week for two terms. This works well if you have a full-time job as you will not need to be without a salary for a month or more and you may be able to work flexi-time or take some annual leave if the pattern of attendance includes an afternoon. Sophia, who had trained as a secondary school teacher in Greece, 'was working at the same time. It was an extremely busy time as I had two part-time jobs at two different colleges.' A part-time course can also suit you if you have other commitments like family as you can try to work these around the demands of the course. Miranda did her certificate part-time and this worked well. 'It was quite hard work and I had to be very organized, but I was working part-time and the children weren't too small, so it was manageable.' Andrea, who has two children and was teaching about 10 hours a week while doing the course, enjoyed it. 'I found it difficult, but doable because there was time from one session to the next to prepare.'

If you are someone who likes time to reflect and think and you do not respond well to working under a lot of pressure, then a part-time course is ideal as it gives you time to absorb new ideas and learn new techniques. Aiden feels that, 'Part-time is better because there's so much to take on board. It's like driving or playing an instrument. There are lots of small parts that you have to practise individually and put them all together to make the whole thing. If you try to rush it, it won't work.' Nathan also prefers the slow gradual immersion. 'I don't see the point in rushing things and doing them badly, unless you really need to.' It is still very hard work, though, and you will need to clear some space in your life to study outside course hours if you want to succeed. You need time to read and to do coursework and assignments as well as plan lessons for the classes you will be teaching. It is important to keep a sense of balance, though, and Liz says, 'I wouldn't say it took over my life, but it was certainly on my mind a lot of the time as I wanted to do as well as I possibly could. I still went to the pub and everything the same as usual.'

6 Specializing and moving up the ladder

After you have got your ELT certificate and taught for a while in Britain or abroad, you need to decide where you want to go with your life and if you want to make teaching your career or whether you want to move on. Jo, who now works in publishing, found that 'The chance to live and work abroad offered me the most amazing opportunity to jump into different cultures and suspend real life for a while.' She taught abroad for five years and then, 'realized that what had started as a year out to think about my career had unwittingly become my career'. When Paul first started teaching, 'It was all new and exciting and I thought, "This is something I can do for the rest of my life",' but both he and Jo decided to leave teaching and move into other jobs.

If you find that you still enjoy teaching after the first novelty has worn off and you feel that it is a career rather than a job, then you may be ready for further training and want to consider an additional specialist qualification or a higher level course. Alan worked in Italy and, 'There was a point when I decided that this was my career. I really wanted to keep doing it as I was enjoying it so much.' He then took an ELT diploma and has gone on to be Head of Training for an international company. Ricky taught in Spain for a number of years and also realized that she needed a further qualification if she wanted to progress. She came back to Britain and did an MA TESOL as well as an ELT diploma and now teaches on a foundation course at a university, trains teachers and writes materials. You may do further training because you want some career development, but you may also want the challenge and excitement of studying and learning again.

Young learners

English for Young Learners (EYL) is an expanding area of ELT and you are likely to teach children at some stage in your working life whether you are in Britain or abroad. Chris, who works for a large international organization, says they are, 'struggling to meet the demand' for EYL teachers and that, 'It's growing in Britain and abroad and the summer camps are getting bigger every year.' There are plenty of exciting job opportunities and, if you enjoy working with children, you may decide that you want to gain a specialist qualification and make EYL your career.

Certificate in English Language Teaching to Young Learners in Language Schools (UCLES CELTYL)

The CELTYL is awarded by UCLES and is modelled on the CELTA. The course was developed in 1998, but is already recognized internationally and very well respected. Melanie, who trains teachers, says that a specialist course is invaluable because, 'It gives you a grounding in practical skills and techniques for teaching young learners and it gives you some confidence.' It is also important for your job prospects if you want to work with children and Chris says, 'It looks good on paper and reassures employers that you know what you are doing.'

If you do not already have an ELT qualification, you can do the CELTYL as a month's intensive course very like the CELTA. If you know that you want to work with children, then it makes sense to do a specialist course at once, but if you want to leave your options open, then you might be better to do a CELTA and then to do a YL extension to the CELTA course. This is a short course that you can do after your CELTA and it means you have a general ELT qualification as well as a specialism, so you will find it very easy to get work teaching students of any age. The YL Extension builds on what you covered in the CELTA and helps you transfer your teaching skills and knowledge about language and learning to working with young learners. Colin taught adults and children in Japan, but found working with young learners the most rewarding and enjoyed working with children. He did the Extension course after the CELTA and, 'found it absolutely fantastic'.

If you want to do a CELTYL, then you need to go abroad or to be already working abroad as that is where most courses are offered and where the largest market is. At the moment there are more Extension courses offered that meet the needs of teachers who have a certificate and some experience, but find themselves teaching young learners as part of their job. As the demand for trained EYL teachers increases, though, more people are deciding that they want to specialize in this area and more CELTYL courses are being offered. Jo runs Extension courses in Portugal and says that most of the trainees already live there although they will help you find accommodation if you go from Britain specially to do the course. You attend the course in the morning and in the afternoon teach practice classes in Portuguese schools. You teach at two levels and work with children between 7 and 11, although you may get the chance to teach primary children as well. Heather works at a centre in Geneva that delivers the course and says that, 'It's very intensive as they start at 8.30 am and go on till 6.00 pm. The children are in French-speaking schools and are either EFL or native speakers who need to maintain their English.'

At the moment there is only one centre in Britain that offers the Extension course. You are offered a part-time teaching contract during the course and work for a month at a children's summer camp and teach in the morning and attend classes in the afternoon. To get the most out of the course, you need to be able to fit into the summer camp and fit in with the children and the other teachers. Chris, who runs it, says, 'It's a residential course, so everyone has to be a happy bunny and get on with everyone else to make it work.' It is a very intensive work and study programme, and he says, 'The timetable can be demanding, but three years of running these courses has produced overwhelmingly positive feedback from candidates.' There are only six places at a time, so there is a lot of competition as it is a good way to work and train at the same time.

Entry requirements

These are set by UCLES and are the same as for the CELTA, but with an additional screening process, which is extremely important for people who are going to be working with children. Andy, who employs EYL teachers, points out that, 'You have a responsibility when dealing with minors, which includes supervision, welfare and the implications of The Children Act, and it's something an EYL teacher must constantly be aware of.' To do a CELTYL Extension course, you have to:

- meet the entry requirements for a CELTA (see previous chapter);

- give your National Teacher Registration number if you have one;

- give the names of three referees who will comment on your suitability to work with young learners and will say if they know of any reason why you should not work in this context;

- sign a self-declaration in which you comment on your suitability to work with young learners.

Centres will interview you and take up your references and, if there is any doubt about your suitability to work with young learners, they will carry out further checks including a police check.

Course content

The content you study on the course covers the same topics as on a CELTA course, but everything you do is directly related to working with children. The course will focus on teaching learners either from 5–10, or 11–16 or 8–13, but you will teach children at the extremes of the age group and work at different levels. You will:

- analyse language and be able to describe how it works;

- find out about how children develop socially, intellectually and emotionally;

- understand how children learn language at different stages of their development;

- prepare and plan lessons that are suitable for young learners;

- develop practical skills for teaching different ages and levels;

- choose and use materials that motivate young learners and are suitable for their needs;

▌ use a variety of activities like art, craft and music to teach children of different ages and at different levels of language;

▌ monitor the children's progress and keep records;

▌ be able to assess and evaluate your own development as a teacher.

Assessment

The CELTYL and the YL Extension course are organized in the same way as the CELTA and are assessed in the same way. If you pass the course, you are awarded a certificate, which is graded A, B or C (although the YL Extension only awards Pass or Fail) and you are assessed throughout the course, so all the work you do contributes to your overall grade. You have to:

▌ produce a number of practical assignments during the course;

▌ watch experienced teachers in the classroom and write up your observations;

▌ be observed teaching for at least six hours (four for the Extension);

▌ teach children of different ages and levels of English.

Costs

The cost of a CELTYL is similar to a CELTA and can be anything from £800 upwards, although an Extension course is shorter so fees will be lower. Costs vary from centre to centre and from country to country, so you need to do some careful research if you decide to go abroad to do your course. If you are already teaching abroad, then you will probably choose to do the course at the centre nearest to you and will not be able to shop around in the same way.

ELT diploma courses

It is worth studying for a diploma if you plan to make a career of ELT as it is usually required for full-time jobs in further education colleges and for more senior posts in private language schools. The British Council, for example, prefers all its teachers to have an ELT diploma and offers salary increments as an incentive. If you are employed by The British Council with only a certificate, you will be encouraged to do a diploma and may get help with fees or reduced teaching hours while you are doing a course. Sean says 'It's worth doing if you want to teach for any length of time,' and Steve agrees that a diploma is, 'definitely worth doing. You see "diploma-level preferred" in the _Times Educational Supplement_ and it sets you up quite nicely.' If you want a job at anything above the level of a main-grade teacher, then you need to think about getting a diploma after you have been teaching for a few years. A diploma is for experienced teachers, so you should already have a certificate and you should have taught full- or part-time for at least a couple of years. James taught abroad for 10 years before coming back to England to do his diploma and says, 'I realized that if I was going to move on in any way and to really know what I was doing, then I would need to get the diploma.'

Like certificate courses, diploma-level courses are offered at FE colleges, universities and the bigger private language schools. You can also study for the DELTA at centres abroad, although this is not yet the case for the Trinity, and both now offer a distance learning route to qualification. The diploma is not eligible for a government grant of any kind, but you may be able to get a tax rebate on the examination entry costs if you study in Britain or to use your Individual Learning Account towards your fees.

UCLES and Trinity diplomas

The two best-known and widely recognized diplomas are the UCLES DELTA (Diploma in English Language Teaching to Adults) and the Trinity Diploma in English Language Teaching. There are more centres offering the DELTA worldwide than the Trinity and, as with the ELT certificate, they tend to be long established centres that have delivered teacher training for many years. Both courses offer high-quality training, though, so the sensible thing is find out what is available at centres near you and to choose a course and mode of study that suits your personal and teaching situation.

Entry requirements

The awarding bodies, ie UCLES or Trinity, set their own entry requirements and the centre offering the course may also have its own additional requirements. You will usually be interviewed and may be asked to do a piece of writing. Generally, you should have:

- a certificate-level qualification;

- considerable recent teaching experience, which may be expressed as a number of years or a number of hours taught;

- degree-entry-level qualifications, although in exceptional cases you may get a place if you are a mature candidate with considerable work experience;

- good study skills and be able to write extended essays following academic conventions;

- experience of teaching at different levels;

- used a variety of ELT materials and resources and be able to talk about them.

Unless you are doing an intensive course on which teaching practice is organized for you, you should be teaching at different levels during the course as you will need to be observed with different classes.

Course content

A diploma course is a mixture of theory and practice. As an experienced teacher you should be able to teach a class using a variety of different methods and aids, but your techniques will be polished during the course and you will be encouraged to try out new approaches and to adapt your teaching to different levels. You will:

- examine some theory about foreign and second language learning and look at the rationale underpinning materials design and classroom practice;

- find out about your learners' needs, aspirations and interests;

- study some theory about lesson and programme planning that you will be expected to apply to your own situation;

- evaluate published materials and resources at different levels and look at ways of using, adapting and supplementing these for a variety of purposes with your learners;

▌ learn more about the language systems of English and be expected to thoroughly research language points using a variety of different grammar books;

▌ look at different ways to present and practise language in the classroom using appropriate materials and methods;

▌ learn how to help learners develop across the four skills of listening, speaking, reading and writing and examine the sub-skills used to carry out different everyday activities;

▌ look at the principles and practicalities of assessment and testing;

▌ explore ways of continuing your own professional development.

Your own teaching forms an important part of the course as you are observed working at different levels and are also expected to reflect on your practice and to write self-evaluations. You will be observed by tutors on the course and may also be watched by other trainees and an external assessor. You will get very detailed verbal and written feedback on your teaching and clear guidance on areas for improvement, which you will be expected to put into practice in the following observation.

Assessment

The courses are similar in that you will be assessed on:

▌ your practical teaching at different levels, which will be observed by your tutors and an external assessor;

▌ written assignments and projects you do during the course, which are marked by your tutors and external examiners;

▌ a three-hour exam, which is externally marked.

Assessment for the Trinity diploma also includes a half-hour interview about phonology with an external examiner in which you demonstrate that you understand how the sound system of English works and that you can teach it in the classroom.

Costs

A diploma course costs anything between £650 and £1,250 at the time of writing, so do shop around. Generally, further education colleges are cheaper than private language schools, but find out what is available near where you live. If you work full-time, your employer may be prepared to contribute to the costs and some colleges may let you pay your fees in instalments, but it is a significant outlay and you also need to budget for books and travel. A diploma is an investment, though, as it is your passport to promotion and to better pay, so it is well worth saving for.

Intensive courses

As with certificate courses, diplomas are offered at further education colleges, universities and the bigger private language schools and you can choose to study in Britain or abroad. An intensive diploma course lasts for about eight weeks and is very hard work as you will be at college full-time attending classes and teaching yourself during the course. You will also have assignments to do in your own time and have to prepare yourself for an exam. John, who did the course over 10 weeks, says, 'I think you have to be incredibly disciplined to get your work done in a small amount of time without feeling overwhelmed, but it was great.'

To get the most from an intensive diploma course, you must be prepared to work very hard and to think and breathe ELT for its duration. Madeleine, who dropped out of a part-time diploma, says, 'I have to do it intensively if I do it at all. I need to know that I'm getting the most out of things at any one time.' As well as attending classes, you will be expected to do additional reading around the course content and to plan your own ELT classes in great detail. Intensive courses work well if you have few outside commitments and your family and friends are supportive and, of course, if you can afford to take two months unpaid leave while you study.

Part-time courses

Part-time courses are generally one or two evenings a week for a year, so you can be working and getting a salary while you are studying. A diploma is an in-service course, which means that you will be teaching full- or part-time while you are studying. This is hard work as going to a three-hour evening class straight after work, missing supper, getting home late and having to get up for work the next morning is tough. Sophia did her diploma part-time and thinks that, 'If you want to become a teacher as a professional, then you certainly need more time because you evolve as a teacher during the course and you can't evolve in two months.'

Sean, who is halfway through his course, finds it, 'a lot of work and it's hard to keep up with the reading', but a part-time course has the advantage of giving you a year to, 'absorb new ideas and use them in lessons'. It also means that you can have a break in the holidays and work at your own pace to some extent and, 'have the chance to experiment'. Rachel was working full-time when she did her diploma two evenings a week, but says, 'It was OK because it was practical, so I was able to use everything I learned straight away. It complemented my work, so I was able to cope.'

A part-time course will suit you if you want to give yourself time to do other things and do not like working under continuous pressure. Andrew, who has a young family and is doing the diploma one evening a week on top of his full-time job, says that, 'The time for the input sessions is not a major issue as I work two evenings a week anyway, but I find the pace quite uneven. I suppose it has to be. There's frantic activity before an assignment and then there's a period of relative calm and then more frantic activity.' Frances, who did a diploma a few years ago says, 'I need a balance in my life and things other than work for me to enjoy myself.'

Distance learning

It is now possible to study for your ELT diploma by distance learning, which means you could study in Britain, if that suits your circumstances better than attending a course, or from abroad if you are living and teaching there. International House London and the British Council jointly offer the UCLES DELTA and a number of centres offer the Trinity diploma. You will need to be teaching full- or part-time while you study as you will have to be observed as part of the course and will have to apply what you learn to your own teaching situation. You will need access to a computer as you will get a CD ROM with course materials and will communicate with your tutor and other trainees by e-mail and have online discussions and seminars. The courses are assessed in exactly the same way as those that are delivered face-to-face, so you have to do written assignments and sit an exam, observe other teachers and be observed yourself teaching at different levels.

Many long distance learners can feel quite lonely and isolated, but there is plenty of support available from tutors and from your fellow trainees who are probably feeling many of the same things as you. You also get the chance to meet your tutors and fellow learners in person at some stage in the course, so they are not just names. A Trinity course usually includes attendance at college in Britain for a two-week block where you are observed teaching and the Distance DELTA involves a two-week orientation course at International House London or one of the regional centres abroad.

Postgraduate Certificate of Education courses

If you are a graduate and want a career in the state sector in Britain, you could do a Postgraduate Certificate of Education course at a university. This is usually one year full-time and the university arranges and supervises your teaching practice at one or more further education colleges. Students often progress to a PGCE immediately after graduating while they are in the habit of full-time study and used to living on a student income and loan.

The course gives you qualified teacher status, which is important if you plan to work in the state education sector as the government is making it mandatory for FE teachers to get a qualification recognized by the Department for Education and Employment. If you want to work in the private sector, language schools generally prefer an ELT certificate or diploma to a PGCE and FE colleges will also require this if your PGCE is in a subject other than ELT.

Entry requirements

You must be a graduate and admission to the course is by interview, although you may also be asked to do some writing. It is useful if you have already done some teaching or at least observed some language classes before you go for interview, as the interviewer will want to ensure that you have some idea of what you are going in to.

Course content

A PGCE is a generic teaching qualification, which gives you the opportunity to specialize in ELT and a subsidiary subject. You will study the theory and practice of ELT, but the course will also include:

▌ learning theory and the psychology of learning;

▌ the development of the FE sector and its place in the British education system;

▌ government policies that shape the FE sector;

▌ roles and responsibilities in FE and professional practice and development.

You usually study some core components with other students teaching a wide variety of other subjects and then divide into an ELT subject specialism for part of the course. There is not nearly as much emphasis on methodology as on certificate or diploma courses and many people feel the need to go on and do one of these after doing a PGCE. Dawn did her certificate after her PGCE and while she was teaching ESOL in an FE college and felt that she, 'learned more about actual teaching in three months than I did in a whole year on my PGCE'. Fiona did her qualifications the other way round and did an intensive ELT course followed by a PGCE, 'because I wanted qualified teacher status and a DfEE number'. She had the same experience as Dawn and, 'learned more about ELT methodology on a month's course than I did on my PGCE', but courses vary and you may feel a PGCE equips you sufficiently. Like Dawn and Fiona you may decide to do a certificate or diploma, which will give you lots of guidance and feedback about methodology in addition to a PGCE that includes ELT.

You will be given a teaching placement in an FE college and will teach under the supervision of an experienced teacher. You generally go to college one day a week during your teaching placement, so you also have the opportunity to discuss your teaching with colleagues and tutors and to relate theory to practice. You will be observed by your tutor and experienced teachers at the placement college and are also expected to reflect on your own practice and learn from it.

Assessment

You will be assessed on your teaching practice and on assignments you do during the course and you may also sit an examination. You will probably also be asked to keep a reflective journal, which will form part of your assessed work. PGCEs are Pass or Fail and, if you are successful, you can apply for full- or part-time work in FE.

Costs

Your course fees will be paid by your local authority and you can apply for a student loan towards your living expenses, but you should be prepared for a year of living frugally while you study and teach.

Moving on up

After you have been working in ELT for some time, you may want to get a further qualification that will enable you to move up the ladder professionally. You may want the opportunity to progress to a post that involves more responsibility, for example a Director of Studies in a private language school, a Curriculum Manager in an FE college or to move into teacher training. It is possible to do this without a further qualification, but to compete successfully you need to obtain a higher-level qualification of some kind.

Specialist ELT courses

There are some specialist qualifications offered in particular areas of ELT such as English for Business and English for Academic Purposes. There may be a course that looks as though it offers exactly what you want, but it is important to find out if the qualification is widely recognized in Britain and abroad. If the course is accredited by Trinity or UCLES, which are the two main awarding bodies in the field of ELT, then it will be widely recognized and will include assessment of your practical teaching. BATQI (the British Association of TESOL Qualifying Institutions) publishes a register of accredited courses and only includes those awarded by a recognized validating body and with substantial supervised teaching practice. If only the college or university offering the course awards the qualification, however, it may not have much currency abroad or even outside the geographical catchment area of the institution.

It is also important to find out how the course is assessed, as it may be that you have to do almost as much work as you would for an MA. If that is the case, you may be better to enrol directly on a Masters that includes modules in the specialism you want to pursue. Alternatively, check that the course offers you credits towards a Masters and make sure you can progress further if you so wish at a later stage.

ELT management courses

ELT management courses are fairly new and are useful if you are working in private language schools and wish to stay in that sector. As yet, they do not have currency in the state sector and you would be better advised to do a generic certificate or diploma in management if you want to progress. In the private sector, though, they are a welcome development as there have been limited career development opportunities in ELT. International House London offers a Diploma in Education Management and a Director of Studies course and, like any management course, they are for experienced teachers wanting to move up the ladder or already in a management role and wanting to get some theory to improve their practice. As these courses are new, you may decide that it is safer to study for one that has international recognition, but an ELT management course will suit you if you are more interested in a practical course that will help you do your job more effectively.

Masters degrees

Universities now offer a wide range of Masters degrees in the field of ELT. Some courses are broad-based and others are very specific, for example, an MA in English for Special Purposes or in English for Young Learners, so you will need to find out the variety of what is on offer and to think carefully about the direction you want your career to take before you decide. It is also important to choose a course in which you have a genuine interest as you will be studying the subject for one or two years of more. Rachel decided to do an MA because she wanted to, 'become more marketable and get some professional development, but I also wanted to broaden my horizons', and the subject does need to be one that fascinates you. The hope of career advancement may not be enough to keep you going during what could be quite a long haul, so find out what is available and choose your MA carefully.

It can be very exciting studying on an MA course as you get the opportunity to learn from some of the big name academics in the field in ELT. You may have read quotes by them or looked at some of their books, but that is very different to doing a seminar with an ELT academic and hearing them talk about their ideas in person. Ricky says that her MA, 'really opened my mind and made me think about theoretical things I hadn't thought about before and I was very fortunate to be studying under brilliant people'. Although you will find it very useful to study something that you can apply to your work, there is still a great pleasure in studying something that interests you for its own sake, so choose an MA that genuinely interests you.

Entry requirements

You should generally have a first degree and have been working in ELT for some years before you do an MA, but some universities may offer the opportunity to go directly into an MA without a first degree if you can demonstrate that you have worked in the field of ELT and have other relevant qualifications like a diploma. If your MA is in Teaching English to Speakers of Other Languages, you may need to have a PGCE or a Certificate of Education or to do an entrance exam. Some universities give you credits towards your MA for having a relevant ELT diploma, but you must check carefully with the institution to which you are applying as each university has discretion over its own entry requirements and these vary.

Mode of study

With an MA, you have the option of:

- studying full-time for a year;
- doing a course part-time over two or more years;
- studying by distance learning over two or more years.

Full-time   If you do a full-time course, you have the luxury of being able to devote your whole energy to your studies and to concentrate fully on what you are learning. This can be an enormous delight after years of teaching where you are always trying to do lots of things at once, but it can be difficult at first if you have not studied for some time. Ricky came back to England to do a full-time MA, but felt, 'It's very intensive doing it full-time and it can feel very theoretical and removed from real life.' Frances chose to study full-time as she had, 'got a bit bogged down with teaching, but it gave me a whole new burst of energy and enthusiasm and I thought about things in a different way'. She was fortunate enough to get a year's unpaid leave from her full-time job and says, 'I loved it. I used to go sometimes to the university library to work on a Saturday and I'd think, "This is bliss. I'm so lucky".'

Full-time study can certainly be a refreshing change if you can afford it and you may be able to do a few hours part-time teaching a week to help financially. If you have been teaching for some time and feel that you need to recharge your batteries again, then it could be worth saving up to do a full-time MA. If you work in Britain, it may be worth talking to your employer about the possibility of unpaid leave and if you have been teaching abroad on a contract that gives you a bonus at the end, then that could be a good way to finance your MA if you decide to come back for a year.

Part-time   The pattern of attendance will vary from institution to institution and you may attend in the evening or a combination of an afternoon or evening over two years. Patrick did his MA part-time over two years while teaching full-time at an FE college and attended university in the evening two or sometimes three times a week. This was hard work on top of a full-time job and he had to be very focused and disciplined to get the work done. He found it difficult to find long enough chunks of time in which to settle down to read and study, but got very good at being able to work in a very concentrated way for short stretches of time during term-time. He was able to use the holidays for wider reading and to write up the research for his dissertation and he also got a few days study leave to revise for his exams. Ricky transferred to a part-time MA, but then found that, 'It seemed to stretch on endlessly,' and some people can take up to four years to complete it. In the end, of course, 'It depends on your situation and your way of learning,' and on your financial commitments and work flexibility.

Distance learning   Many MAs are now offered by distance learning, which means that you can choose a course that interests you and study it from anywhere in Britain or abroad as long as you have access to a computer. Rachel, who works full-time and has a young son, chose a distance learning MA because she thought, 'It would fit in better with my lifestyle as I wouldn't have to go anywhere.' Her MA is fairly structured, which suits her as, 'It makes you do something every week,' and she is given reading to do, which she then has to discuss via e-mail with her tutor group. She says, 'It's almost better than a seminar because everyone has to participate equally,' and they then get tutor feedback on their discussion. Rachel never meets her fellow learners face-to-face, but is studying with people from all over the world. One student works for an oil company in Angola for half the year and is back in Britain for the other half, so distance learning is ideal for him. Other students come from Canada, Brunei, Japan, Turkey, Korea, the Middle East and Britain, so a distance learning MA is a very good way to get an international perspective on ELT.

Not all distance learning MAs are organized in exactly the same way, of course, so it is important to choose one that fits in with your lifestyle and teaching situation. Keith is now back in Britain, but he was working in Sri Lanka when he started his MA in ELT management. He says, 'I was fired up for the first couple of years, but it's actually harder now I'm back here.' Like Rachel, he had e-mail contact with his tutors and with other learners all over the world and he found the course, 'very good as it focused on the job you were doing'. Everyone on his course, wherever they were in the world had to come to England every six months to the university where they had a residential programme and met each other. Keith had been working abroad for nearly 10 years by the time he began his MA and he liked the face-to-face contact with other ELT professionals in similar positions. 'It was expensive, but very good as you met people.' Now that he is teaching back in Britain, that is not so important and he has found it quite difficult to start his studies again, so it is important to try to match your MA to your needs as well as your interests.

Course content

The course content will obviously vary depending on whether your course is broad-based or more specialized, but MAs are academic rather than practical. If you do an MA in ELT you will study different theories about language, how it works and how people learn it. You will learn to analyse language in different ways and look at the ways English has changed and is changing and its role as a world language. MAs do not focus on the methods and materials of practical teaching in the same way as a diploma course, although Rachel has found that she is, 'certainly able to relate it to my teaching'. You must be prepared to read very widely across your field and to carry out some research yourself as part of your MA. Although you may be teaching part-time during your course, observation of teaching practice will not form any part of the programme although you may look at different ways of analysing and describing the interactions in language classrooms.

Assessment

To pass your MA, you are assessed on your ability to:

▨ write assignments on set topics;

▨ read widely and participate in seminars in person or by e-mail if you do a distance learning course;

▨ research and write up a dissertation, usually at least 20,000 words, on a topic agreed with your tutor.

You usually have to sit an exam or exams at some stage of your course. Unlike a first degree, an MA is not usually graded but your dissertation may be awarded a Pass or Distinction.

Costs

An MA is a major financial commitment as it costs at least £2,500–3,500 and you have to buy books on top of that. If you are working full-time, your employer may contribute to the fees and you may also be able to pay in instalments. There are some very limited sources of discretionary funding available, but you need to apply early and have a very good first degree (generally a first) to be considered for an award, so it is best to start saving well before you begin your MA.

7 Getting your first ELT job

Where to look

There are plenty of ELT jobs available in Britain and abroad and a variety of ways of finding out about them. Sometimes you might be lucky enough to be in the right place at the right time to hear about a job before it is advertised, but generally, you will have to look for vacancies yourself and apply.

Newspapers

If you are applying from Britain, the best place to look for ELT jobs is in the national press where jobs in the state and private sector in Britain and abroad are advertised throughout the year. There is a lot of EFL work available at Easter and short-term contracts start being advertised from late January. There is even more teaching available in the summer when students come over on short courses of three weeks or a month, so it is worth starting to look from before Easter. Most summer or Easter schools employ additional teachers on temporary contracts, which is a good way of getting experience when you are starting out. The courses are quite fun too, as students are here to have a holiday as well as learn English, so there is usually a lively social programme. All of the national papers have their own Web sites and you can access the job pages via the Internet if you prefer.

The *Times Educational Supplement*, which comes out on Fridays, is the most obvious place to start as it offers jobs across the ELT field. It is divided into different sections for schools, further, adult and higher education and has a separate TEFL listing. Full- and part-time jobs are advertised and so are short summer or Easter contracts. It includes jobs in Britain and abroad and within both the state and private sectors.

The Education section of _The Guardian_, which appears on a Tuesday, also has a very good, large TEFL section and includes private language schools and further and adult education colleges. The job section of _The Guardian_ on Saturday also includes a TEFL section. _The Independent_ on Thursday covers jobs in education and includes some ELT.

If you want to work teaching ESOL to local residents and refugees in your area, then it is also worth looking in your local paper, which may carry advertisements for part-time or voluntary work in adult education or with community groups. The advertisements can appear at any time, but there are usually many jobs in the state sector advertised in May. People have to give in their notice by the end of May if they plan to start a new job in September, so this is a particularly good time to start looking for work.

Recruitment agencies

If you know you want to work abroad, then you could also try using one of the ELT recruitment agencies, which fill positions all year round. They are generally looking for people with a recognized ELT qualification like the CELTA or Trinity, so it is not worth applying after an introductory course. Some agencies recruit only for their own schools and others recruit for their own schools as well as client schools all over the world. You do not have to see a particular job advertised, but can contact the agency with your details and say where you would like to work. This can work well if you know you want to work in a particular country and there is certainly a huge demand for teachers in Eastern Europe and the Far East at the moment.

The big recruitment agencies advertise in the ELT jobs sections of the newspapers, but they also have their own Web sites and you can find out about what jobs are available and how to apply. Some agencies hold open days in centres all over the country and provide information and the chance to talk informally to people who have worked in different countries. Again, these events are advertised and you can usually just turn up and some even interview on the day, although you may want the chance to find out some information and go for an interview on another occasion.

Contacts

If you are looking to start work immediately after doing an ELT certificate or a PGCE in Britain, the institution at which you studied may also be able to provide you with contacts. For example, if you do a PGCE it is worth keeping in touch with the college where you do your teaching practice so that you hear about vacancies that arise in the future. Some private language schools that deliver teacher training guarantee you employment at one of their schools if you get a 'B' or above for your ELT certificate. The big private schools are also part of chains and have their own Web sites, which are regularly updated with news of short- and long-term vacancies at their schools in Britain and abroad. If you do an ELT certificate, it is also worth keeping in touch with the school or college as there is often a need for teachers at short notice to staff an extra class or to cover for absent colleagues. This will not lead directly to a full- or part-time job, but it puts you in a good position to hear about work and lets the school know that you are available.

Just turning up abroad

If you live in Britain and are moving into the world of ELT because you want to work abroad, the most sensible thing to do is apply for a job and get all the details of your contract, flights, medical insurance and accommodation sorted out before you go. For a variety of reasons, though, you might already be abroad and in a position to start looking for ELT work. You might live abroad, like Pam, and start teaching as a way of funding your studies; you might be travelling like James and want to use ELT to pay your way, or you might have done your ELT certificate abroad like Sean and decide to stay on. They all found ELT opportunities without any difficulty and it is certainly still possible to get work abroad if you just turn up and look for teaching jobs when you get there.

There are various ways of finding ELT jobs once you are abroad and Roger of International House says that, 'Turning up on the spot can still be very effective. You might be lucky enough to walk into a school and meet a director who likes you and thinks, "She'll fit in beautifully here." They often like that because it means they've met you, whereas they don't know who they're getting when they go through an agency.' Simon, who had done an ELT certificate, says that, 'I just turned up in Madrid and walked round the schools. I got a job in one of the first ones I walked into.' If you are qualified and want to just turn up abroad and try for work, then do make sure you take photocopies of your qualification certificates with you so that you can produce these if you are asked.

If you are trying to get ELT work without a teaching qualification while living or travelling abroad, opportunities often arise by word of mouth as you meet people who may then ask you to do some teaching. John was a qualified secondary school teacher, but had no ELT qualification. He just turned up in the Canaries and got his first job after he, 'got chatting to a guy in a bar who introduced me to the head of the dodgy language school he had studied at. I was teaching a class within an hour.'

You could also try advertising yourself as a private tutor, which is what Simon did in Argentina where he put an advertisement in the local English newspaper and got his first private students. You should also check whether there are private tutoring agencies with which you could register and also look in the jobs section of the local paper in the town or city where you live. Adrian does not have an ELT qualification, but he got his first job in a small language school soon after arriving in Spain. He, 'browsed through the yellow pages mailing my CV to all and sundry' and says that although, 'schools usually state a preference for TEFL people, they'll readily accept graduates'. Pam lives in Germany and has been teaching for some time and she finds that, 'Even the bigger language schools like Berlitz and Inlingua take native speakers without ELT qualifications.'

Whether or not you have an ELT qualification, there are still plenty of teaching opportunities abroad and a variety of strategies you can use to find work:

- responding to advertisements in the local paper or on notice-boards;

- placing advertisements yourself in the local English newspaper or even on trees like Andrew did in Israel;

- cold-calling language schools like Adrian in Spain;

- using word of mouth, which means telling everyone you meet that you are looking for ELT work and being prepared to follow up leads and connections.

It is often a case of being in the right place at the right time and you may be lucky enough to get an ELT job at once like Simon in Spain or James in Iran. You may also need to do a lot of hard work and to be very persistent as the job market varies from country to country and getting enough work to live on is not always easy. Andrew was living in Israel when he moved into ELT, but says that, 'It took me a long time to get a job as it's a difficult job market to break into there.' Job availability will vary according to the season and school terms begin at different times in different parts of the world, so make sure you have enough money to survive on for a while if you do not get a job at once.

Your application

You may be lucky like Andrea who teaches part-time in London and says, 'I haven't had to look for work at all. I've been offered things as I've gone along,' but most teachers have to be prepared to spend some time applying for jobs. If you have not applied for a job before or if this is the first application for some time, then it is worth getting some specialist advice about how to present your CV and fill in an application form. Some ELT courses will include a session on this and, if you take your certificate at a state college, it will have a Careers Centre, which will be able to offer lots of practical tips. If you are a recent graduate, then your university Careers Service will also be able to help you. There are also a number of good books on the market, which offer advice on the whole process of job application and it may be worth investing in one of these.

Cold-calling

Most teachers apply for ELT jobs by responding to an advertisement placed by a school or recruitment agency, but you can also do what is known as 'cold-calling'. This means sending the following to schools and agencies:

- your CV;
- a covering letter with information about yourself and what you can do;
- a smiling passport-type picture of yourself in business dress.

Andrew was applying for work in Britain in the autumn immediately after completing his ELT certificate and had been told it would be impossible to get a job, because it was just after the summer and most schools would have quietened down. As a former estate agent, he was good at selling things and decided he needed to sell himself to get work. 'I employed sales tactics. I sent off CVs and then I phoned up language schools and asked for the Director of Studies' name. I then waited a day and phoned up and gave my name. I very confidently asked for them by name and got put through. I got three interviews and was offered two jobs, so it worked.' You need to be persistent if you decide to use cold-calling and it is important to follow up your initial application with a phone call reminding the organization that you have sent your details and that you are still looking for work.

General advice

If you are applying for an advertised job, it is important to apply in the way the organization asks you to, as ignoring their instructions can mean that they will not even look at your application. Some schools and colleges ask you to phone or e-mail and some of the large organizations have their vacancy list and application form on their Web site, so the initial process of application is carried out using the Internet. Many employers, though, still ask you to send a CV or to complete an application form. Either way, you should always include a supporting statement and a polite covering letter with your application. Conventions of CV presentation vary, but you should produce your CV on no more than two sheets of A4 and have copies available to send to prospective employers if you decide to apply 'cold' by sending your details to private language schools or FE colleges.

The application form

You will have filled in many forms of one kind or another and may have successfully applied for a number of jobs, but as you are moving into ELT, which is a new departure, it is worth reminding yourself of the sensible way to approach the job application form. If you are filling in a paper version, some basic general advice about completing a job application form is to:

Make one or two copies of the blank form before you start in case you make a mistake and need to start again.

Fill in the form in pencil first and carefully check how it looks before you begin to write in ink (carefully rub out the pencil afterwards).

Do not use correction fluid or crossings out on your application, but start a new form if you make a mistake.

Use black ink as the organization will probably want to copy the form.

Make sure you follow the instructions on the form and present the information in the order in which it is required, eg list your education chronologically or with the most recent first.

Make a copy of the completed form so you know what you have said.

Tell the truth as it is a very serious offence to lie on an application form and you could be sacked if they offer you the job on the basis of untrue information. You could also be found out at interview if they ask you questions. For example, do not say you can speak Spanish if you can say nothing more than, 'Hola', as one of the interviewers may speak to you in Spanish and you will immediately be exposed as a fraud.

Check that you have the correct details of anyone you give as a referee and make sure they are happy to act in this capacity for you (if you have recently done an ELT course, then your tutor will give you a reference).

Send the form in good time to meet the closing date and send it recorded delivery so you are sure it arrives safely.

Supporting statement

You should include a supporting statement with your application in which you show how your qualifications and experience match the demands of the advertised job or the organization or country if you are applying 'cold'. You should:

▌ Word-process your statement.

▌ Keep it to no more than two sides of A4.

▌ Put your name at the top and include the job reference if there is one.

▌ Use relevant headings to present information about yourself.

▌ Explain how your skills and experience will benefit the organization.

▌ Link your statement to the experience and skills asked for in the job details.

▌ Give concrete examples that show you have the qualities and experience you claim, eg 'I am a good organizer and ran an after school club for… '.

▌ Say why you want to move into ELT if you are making a career shift.

▌ Say when you are available to start work. Neil interviews a lot of candidates for jobs in Britain and abroad and says that he is often looking for teachers at short notice, so availability is crucial.

▌ Keep a copy of your statement.

Although there are lots of ELT jobs available, you may have to apply for a number of them before you strike lucky and are called for interview. This is common, so you must not feel dispirited if you are not immediately successful.

Preparing for the interview

Interviews are always rather stressful, particularly when you very much want the job or if you have been looking for some time and have not yet been successful, but thorough preparation will help you feel more confident. Before the interview, you should:

▍ Predict the kind of questions you are likely to be asked about your background and experience.

▍ Prepare thoroughly by thinking of what you would like to say to present yourself in the best light.

▍ If ELT is a change of career for you, then be prepared to say why you are giving up your old career. It is important to make this a positive statement about ELT rather than being negative about earlier employment.

▍ Persuade a friend or someone you trust to role-play the interview with you; give them the questions and practise your answers.

▍ Be prepared to give concrete examples of things you claim you can do, eg 'I'm particularly interested in producing my own materials and have recently made a pack about using public transport in London using authentic materials.'

▍ Give specific examples of published materials you have used (and be ready to give your opinion of them) or of materials you have made.

▍ Be prepared to talk about classes and students you have taught at different levels (this can be during the teaching practice on your initial training course) and with different language backgrounds.

▍ Know why you want the particular job for which you are applying. You may want a job, any job in fact, but it is not politic to say this at your interview so make sure you think of a reason that relates to the organization or the kind of students you will be working with, eg 'I've been interested in Chinese culture for a long time and I'd like to work for you because it gives me the opportunity to… ' or 'I'd like to work with refugees and asylum seekers because I can see how important it is that they learn the English they need to… '.

▌ Find out something about the language, culture and customs if you applying to work in a particular country abroad.

Some schools will ask you take along a sample lesson plan or some materials when you go for interview as this is clear evidence of what you can do. Georgie employs ELT staff in the state sector and is the Head of Centre at an institute in London and asks short-listed candidates to bring a lesson plan, which they then talk through at interview. She says, 'You'd be amazed at how useful this is as it tells you so much about the candidate. Some turn up with something scribbled on the back of an envelope, so it's obvious they don't do much preparation for anything and don't think things through. Others show they've taken the interview seriously and turn up with a beautifully detailed plan, which spells everything out, and they can talk about what they did and why.' If you are asked to take a lesson plan, it is sensible to:

▌ Take a lesson plan you have actually taught so you can talk about what you did, how it worked and anything you would change next time.

▌ Word-process your lesson plan and set it out so that it is easy to follow who does what, the timings and the order of activities.

▌ Take at least two copies of your plan so that both you and the interviewer(s) can have a copy.

You may be asked to prepare a practical task before the interview. Some organizations will send you a pre-interview task, which may look at an aspect of language, and ask you to think about how you would teach it at different levels. It is also possible that you may be asked to prepare to teach a class or part of a class as part of the selection process. When Josephine went for an interview in Spain, she had to teach a demonstration class to a group of students she had never seen. She had been given some basic information to enable her to prepare the lesson, but she taught for about 20 minutes and was observed by the Director of Studies. It is always difficult to teach a group of students you have never seen before and particularly difficult if you are being observed. She says, 'It was fairly nerve-wracking, but I got the job.' She did not have an

ELT qualification, but had looked at some books and talked to a friend who was a teacher, so perhaps she was lucky.

You may also be asked to take along examples of teaching materials you have used or adapted. Neil, who recruits teachers for a well-established chain with schools all over the world, asks candidates to bring materials when he interviews them face to face and to talk about materials they have used when he interviews by phone. He says, 'It shows me how up-to-date they are and whether they can explain things clearly.' If you are asked to do this, you need to:

▌ Take some materials that you have recently used successfully so that you can talk about why you chose them for your part-icular students and how you used them.

▌ Photocopy two copies of the materials or take the book and a copy (make sure you acknowledge copyright by saying where the materials are from).

▌ Be prepared to evaluate the materials and say what you like and do not like and why or to talk about how you adapted the materials and why.

▌ Show that you understand and can explain the particular piece of language the materials present or practise.

The interview

Although interviews are not a foolproof way of selecting the right person for the job, they are still commonly used. Neil uses the interview to find out, 'how excited the person is about teaching. If they're interested in teaching, they'll be an interesting teacher.' He is looking to find out what experience the candidate has, but also, 'what they've got out of it and whether they've learnt anything from what they've done'. Roger, who has also interviewed teachers for jobs in Britain and abroad, is also looking for, 'some kind of confidence and presence. They've got to believe in themselves and have got to convince me because they've got to convince the students. They've also got to be not just knowledgeable about grammar, which is important, but they've got to be interested in language and want to talk about it.'

As well as showing that you know your subject and that you can teach it, you also have to show the interviewer that you will actually deliver on the job. Georgie has interviewed a lot of teachers over the years and says that, 'It doesn't matter how much someone knows about language and what an engaging personality they have, if they're not going to be reliable. I want someone reliable who's going to turn up for class on time and do the job. They've got to be there.' This is a hard thing to demonstrate at interview, but it helps if you do what you are asked to do by turning up in good time and by taking with you anything that you have been asked to bring like lesson plans or copies of certificates. If you have worked before, your previous employer will be asked to comment on your sickness and lateness record to assure your potential employer that you turn up and do the job.

You may be given a practical task to do when you get to the interview itself. Annette works in ELT recruitment for a very large company with schools all over the world and explains, 'We ask people to produce a lesson plan. We give them three pages from a coursebook and then 20 minutes to prepare a lesson plan from that and then we talk it through with them.' You will probably never have seen the materials before, but the task is a realistic one as, once you are teaching five or more hours a day, you will not have more than 20 minutes to plan a lesson so it demonstrates that you can produce something sensible under pressure. You may also be asked some questions about your knowledge of grammar during the interview and about how you would present different points to students at different levels. Annette says, 'We ask some grammar questions, but we don't go heavily into it if they're newly qualified as they can't be expected to know the whole of English grammar.'

It is important to remind yourself that interviews are a two-way process, which allows you and your potential employer to find out if there is a good match between your skills and abilities and the demands of the job. Paul works in ELT recruitment for the overseas market and says that, 'Basically, we're looking for someone who's sensible, adaptable and flexible enough to translate what they've learnt into teaching in different situations. We're looking to see if they've got the knowledge and confidence to cope in a different situation.' Georgie, who has worked in ELT almost since the beginning and now employs teachers in the state sector in Britain, agrees. 'I'm looking for someone who has done or can do different things. I want a teacher who can do General English, but who could also do Business English or teach English for tourism. In other words, someone who isn't stuck in one thing and can adapt to a changing situation.' The employer wants to find out if you will fit in with the organization and be able to do the job and you need to find out if the job is one you think you can do and would enjoy.

A great deal of time is invested in the recruitment and selection process both by you and by the organization that may employ you. Thorough preparation and good presentation are important to make sure that this time is not wasted. Colin, who recruits teachers who want to work abroad, says, 'We're looking for someone who's prepared to put in the time and effort to get on top of the game.' Any interviewer is also looking for evidence that you have researched the company or certainly the country they are being interviewed for. He says, 'We're looking for cultural awareness and will ask about that.' The rules about what is appropriate to wear may be different depending on whether you are being interviewed in Britain or abroad, but Colin says that, 'Presentation is always very important.' Something casual but smart would probably be appropriate for a private language school or FE college in Britain whereas something more formal may be called for in some cultures, for example, Japan. As a general rule, it is safer to be slightly too formal than to be too casual, which looks to employers as though you are not taking the job seriously.

The big day

On the day of the interview you are bound to feel nervous, but there are things you can do to help you perform to your best and show that your skills and qualities match the demands of the job:

- Go to bed early the night before so you are fresh on the day.

- Decide what to wear and get it ready the night before. Wear something smart, but nothing that makes you feel uncomfortable.

- Eat something for breakfast – you may not feel like it but it will actually make you feel better and will stop your stomach rumbling during the interview.

- Leave plenty of time for your journey so that you will still arrive in good time even if there is a problem with transport.

- Take a copy of your application form, supporting statement and CV with you to the interview.

- Take two copies of a lesson plan or some materials you have made and be prepared to talk about how you used them.

- Take some deep breaths before you go into the interview to calm you down.

- Smile and try to be friendly.

- Make eye contact with the person who has asked you a question.

- Avoid fidgeting, so that you appear calm and confident even if you do not feel it.

- Give full answers with concrete examples, so that you avoid just 'yes' or 'no'.

- Make it clear that you want the particular job offered even if you have applied for lots of others.

- Talk positively about your skills and experience. Sell yourself, but never lie as you are very likely to be caught.

- Ask some questions about the job or organization to show that you are interested, but avoid immediately asking about the pay or holidays (you can find out about these if you are offered the job).

- Find out when they will let you know the outcome of the interview.

- Thank them for interviewing you.

Interviews by phone

It is also possible that you will be interviewed by telephone. If you are applying to work abroad, someone may fly over to interview applicants in person but it is cheaper for them to interview you by phone. The phone could ring at any time, so careful preparation will help you feel more able to present yourself in the best possible light. Alex got a job in Italy without a face-to-face interview. She had answered an advertisement in the paper and sent her CV and some sample lesson plans, but heard nothing at first, 'Then one day I got a phone call and she talked to me briefly on the phone. They needed someone, so that was that.' She later discovered that, 'Someone had left suddenly and they desperately needed a teacher, so I was very last minute.' Alex was fortunate as they paid her flight and flew her out that week and Sean had a similar experience when he got a job in Poland. He was interviewed by phone and offered the job if he could start within three days. They organized flights and, 'All I had to do was pack and get to the airport on time. I flew in and started teaching the next day as they were desperate.'

It is not only schools abroad that interview by phone. Tony runs his own school and takes on extra staff for residential summer courses and he interviews applicants by phone if they meet his basic requirements in terms of qualifications and experience. What he is looking for, in addition to someone with a knowledge of the language they are going to teach is someone who, 'knows what they're doing and whose personality comes across. If they can't engage me over the phone, they're not going to be able to engage a class of students.' Be prepared to give concrete examples of lessons you have taught and materials you have used and to explain how you would present aspects of language at different levels and make sure you sound enthusiastic about teaching.

After the interview

Most people are not offered the first ELT job for which they are interviewed, so do not take it personally if you are not immediately successful. Try to regard interviews as useful practice and experience and think about what you can learn from them. After the interview, review your own answers and think about questions you did not answer as fully as you could have done. Rethink what you could have said and plan how you could improve your performance next time. Many organizations are also prepared to give you informal feedback, which can be very helpful, so it is worth overcoming any embarrassment and phoning to ask if they are prepared to discuss your interview.

Your first ELT job

Congratulations! Your application was successful and you have been offered your first ELT job. This can be quite scary as there is a big difference between doing supervised teaching practice on a certificate course and teaching your own classes on a regular basis. If you have been offered work without having done a course, this can be even scarier as you are now going to have to teach an ESOL or EFL class for the first time. The key thing to remember, though, is that your employer believes you have the experience and skills to do the job so it is up to you enjoy the opportunity and show that the belief is justified.

Preparation

Starting a new job is both exciting and nerve-wracking whether it is your first 'proper' job after being a student or the first in your new career. It helps if you can do some preparation to make you feel more confident, so that you are able to enjoy the first few days and get the most out of the opportunity. You may have been to the place where you will work when you were interviewed, so you know how to get there and how long your journey to work will take. If not, then it is worth finding out exactly where the school is before you start and leaving extra time for your journey on the first day.

The more you can find out before you start, the better prepared you can be, which will help make you feel more confident and less anxious for the first couple of days until you start to find your feet and get to know people. If you can, arrange for someone to show you around before your first teaching day so you can find out and make notes about some key things like:

- the name of the school receptionist or secretary;
- whether you are expected to take registers and where they are kept;
- where the photocopier is and how to use it;
- where additional resource books and materials are kept;
- where to get a tape-recorder and copies of tapes;

- where to get board pens and a rubber;
- which book(s) your class is using;
- where to get a copy of the Teacher's Book.

Some language classes run by adult education or community groups may be very poorly resourced and held in church halls or portacabins, so it is best to find out as much as you can before you start and be prepared for the fact that:

- There may not be a board in the classroom and you may have to use a flipchart (if there is one).

- You may have to provide your own board pens.

- You may have to take your own tape-recorder.

- The centre may not have any of its own resources and you may have to buy your own copies of books you want to use.

- You may have to do your own photocopying and sell copies of handouts to students.

- Students may not be able to afford books and you are expected to produce your own materials.

Ice-breakers

It is exciting to get your first ELT job, but it can be quite stressful suddenly being expected to teach lots of classes without close supervision. You might feel a little nervous about meeting your students for the first time and they might also be nervous about meeting you and each other. To help everyone feel more relaxed it is a good idea to include an ice-breaker activity in your first class to help you and your students get to know each other and learn each other's names. It is certainly worth getting your students to make big name labels to put on their desks (or to pin on themselves if there are no desks in your classroom) and to make yourself a seating plan for the first few days. Go round the class asking students to say their names for you and checking that you pro-nounce them correctly and write down their names (or a 'sounds-like' version) on a sheet of paper according to where they are sitting.

If you did a training course, you will already have some ideas for ice-breaker activities you can use and you may want to use a few of these in the first lessons. If ice-breakers are new to you, then at least put the students into pairs and get them to find out the following from their partner:

▊ name;

▊ where they come from (if you are teaching abroad where all the students are from the same country, substitute another question of your own);

▊ a hobby or interest;

▊ a favourite colour or food.

Of course you can substitute your own questions, but be careful to keep them fairly neutral as students may not feel comfortable sharing too much personal information about themselves. Then get each person to introduce their partner to the rest of the class. At the end of the activity, go round the class and get everyone to say each other's names aloud. You can do this a couple of times and get faster each time to make it fun, as repetition will help the students and you learn each other's names.

Lesson planning

If you have done an ELT training course, you will already know how long it takes to plan lessons and you probably spent hours planning a half-hour lesson. Roger, who trains and employs teachers, points out that, 'You only teach six hours on a course and in a job you'll probably teach five hours in a day, so you just can't do that or you're going to die. There aren't enough hours in the day.' The more you can prepare before you start work the better. Neil, who recruits teachers for Britain and abroad, says, 'The first three months of teaching will be very hard work and you could be working double the hours you're paid.' Find out as much as you can about the level of the class or classes you will be teaching, if they are working towards an exam (and if so which one) and whether they are using a coursebook. If you have access to the Internet, there are a number of good Web sites where you can access free lessons and activities every week from a huge bank of lessons at different levels. They are based around very topical materials and give step by step guidance about what to do and how to use them to teach particular skills or language points, so you can have at least one or two lessons a week that you do not have to plan yourself.

If it is at all possible, try to talk to their previous teacher and find out what they have already done. If that is not possible, then do a variety of different activities during the first few lessons to help you find out about the needs, interests and level of the class. When you first start teaching you will probably spend your evenings planning lessons, but you need to think of ways of making sure you are prepared without giving yourself a nervous breakdown through overwork. If you have just finished a training course, then Alex recommends that you, 'Use any of the lessons that worked particularly well on teaching practice and use those as something you can trust.' Even if the level is not quite right, you might be able to adjust your materials up or down a little, by including some extra activities for a slightly higher level or going through the materials a little more slowly at a lower level. You will find that you are able to plan lessons more quickly as you gain experience, but remember to keep anything you use that works as you can use it again later.

Materials

Most EFL classes use a coursebook on a regular basis and most of the popular ones include additional photocopiable resource materials and have a Teacher's Book to accompany them. Roger says that, 'A lot of people move right away from coursebooks and think they've got to design and produce everything themselves, which is madness.' He advises new teachers to, 'Use the coursebooks as they give you a really sound basis from which you can adapt. Nothing will ever fit your class exactly, but don't waste time re-inventing the wheel. Change the topic or the activity, but use what's already available.' A good Teacher's Book is a lifesaver when you first start teaching as it tells you how to use the materials and gives you ideas about how to supplement the material and use it in different ways.

Most ESOL classes do not use a coursebook and you are expected to produce your own materials. This may be fine if you start by teaching only a couple of hours a week, but you will not have time to produce everything yourself and it is not sensible to try to do so. Ask at the centre or centres where you work and find out if there is already a bank of photocopiable materials you can use and where other resource materials are kept. Even if you decide that you cannot use the materials exactly as they are, you can adapt them slightly and this will still take far less preparation time than starting from scratch.

If there are no materials available, then spend some time in a good ELT bookshop looking at materials and invest in some of your own to start you off. Books of games are a very versatile resource as it is always worth having some 'filler' activities to use up an unexpected 10 minutes at the end of a lesson or to liven things up when the students are getting tired. You might also invest in a couple of the photocopiable resource books that accompany the newer ELT courses as these are collections of speaking, reading and writing activities that can be used on their own even if you are not following the coursebook. Find out if there is a syllabus for the class and as much as you can about their level. Most ESOL classes will be working towards some kind of accreditation, so you will need to find out what it is. Often it will involve students collecting a portfolio of work as evidence of language competencies in speaking, listening, reading and writing, so make sure you find out what record-keeping you are expected to do.

Getting the most out of the job

Starting a new job is hard work, but treat it as an opportunity to learn and you will find that you get a lot more out of the experience. You will start to enjoy the job as you get to know your colleagues and the students, so find out what happens about breaks and use these to get to know people. In some ESOL classes, there is a kettle and you make tea or coffee and spend the break with your students. Large schools and colleges will have their own canteen shared by teachers and students and there will also be a staffroom where you can make a drink and talk to other teachers. In other places, teachers and students go out to a café in the break or at lunchtime, so find out what other teachers do and where they go.

You should also seize the opportunity to learn as much as you can from more experienced teachers. Obviously, you do not want to make a nuisance of yourself, but do not be afraid to ask questions and remember that everyone was a new teacher at some stage. Roger says that, 'You should never be frightened of asking for ideas and being up front and saying, 'Help me, I'm stuck.' Find out about materials that other teachers use and, 'Pinch everything you can get your hands on from other people,' and spend time looking at any resources available at the centre where you work. Large organizations will usually organize an induction programme for new teachers and may even have a mentoring system in place to help you settle in. Roger suggests that, 'If a more experienced colleague says, "I did this and it worked" don't question it, but go and do it as well.' Everybody was new once and teachers are often quite happy to exchange resources and ideas, so use the opportunity to share materials and get to know your colleagues.

If you are part-time it may be more difficult and you will first need to find out if there is a desk you can use, whether you need a key for the staffroom or resources room and if and how you can get photocopying done. Andrea warns that, 'If you're not careful, you can become quite isolated and it can be quite lonely, which isn't really good for you or your teaching.' If you can, try to avoid just arriving, doing your class and going straight home, and give yourself time to chat to the students as they arrive and leave. Neil, a very experienced teacher, advises, 'Enjoy spending time with your students as this takes the edge off things,' but Andrea also stresses the importance of contact with other teachers. Even if you are part-time, you may share classes and you can get the phone number or e-mail address of your co-teacher. She suggests you should, 'Ask lots of questions of experienced teachers and ask if you can observe them if possible.'

Whether you are full- or part-time and whether you are teaching in Britain or abroad, it will be hard work in your first job. There are bound to be days when you feel everything is going wrong and you wonder why you got into ELT in the first place. You are bound to make mistakes, but Rachel, who now trains teachers as well as teaches herself says, 'Don't be too hard on yourself and remember that you're learning. You're not going to be perfect, so don't be afraid to ask for advice from colleagues.' It is important to remember that you chose to work in ELT because it is what you want to do, so learn from things that go wrong and notice that things are going well too. Get the most out of your first job and enjoy it.

8 Related careers

Many people train as English language teachers because they are good at languages and teaching seems an obvious way to use their skills. Some people then discover that they become less interested in teaching and more interested in pursuing other careers that use their language skills and their knowledge of ELT in more tangential ways. Jo had taught in Britain and abroad for a number of years and, 'had started to get bored. I wanted to try to use other skills again.' You could have all sorts of reasons for wanting to move out of language teaching. If you have been teaching abroad for a while, you might want to come back to Britain and be looking for a change of direction like Phiona. For her, 'Most of the advantages of ELT are in working abroad, but I met a guy and wanted to settle back in the UK.'

Jackie, who taught ESOL in the state sector in Britain, felt that, 'I'd been doing ELT for about 15 years and I was looking for a change. I was losing my creativity in ESOL and I wanted something else where I could use that and where I could build on my knowledge.' You may not want to leave teaching completely and may just be looking for other work to stimulate you and stop you feeling stale and bored. Jackie decided to train as a dyslexia specialist and now spends half her timetable providing one-to-one support and the other half still teaching ESOL and says she feels, 'much better about my work in general'.

If you work in the private sector, you may also be tired of, 'low pay, insecurity, dodgy employers and the annual scrabble for the best jobs'. Debbie, who had taught in Britain and abroad, felt she had, 'little job security or possibility to develop further and wanted more development in my career'. Sarah, who taught abroad until she was in her early 30s, looked around at some of her fellow teachers and thought, 'hang on a minute. The ones in their 40s don't look very happy. I don't want to get any older in it.' Whatever your reasons for wanting to get out of teaching, there are a number of possibilities like:

- ELT publishing;

- translation work;

- dyslexia support;

- working in ELT recruitment;

- IT training.

These are all areas are where you will be able to use the communication skills, creativity and knowledge about language, which you have developed in ELT, to do something different.

Working in publishing

Many language teachers do make the move into publishing in one capacity or another and Phiona, who has recently moved into the business, says that ELT publishing is, 'full of ex-TEFL folk with interesting stories to tell'. The wish to move into ELT publishing is understandable and Sarah, who taught in colleges and universities abroad before, admits that, 'It does have a certain amount of status attached to it, which teaching doesn't generally.' Phiona points out that, 'You can always leave a teaching job and go travelling, but jobs in publishing are more coveted and harder to come by.'

You need to choose carefully to find the area of publishing that you think will suit you as there is a lot of choice. For example, you could work in production, marketing, editorial or sales so it is important to know what you like and what you are good at. Debbie, who has worked on a number of projects in publishing, says that, 'If you like working with people and have lots of creative ideas then sales and marketing is a good area. If you have a good eye for detail and like being in an office, then editorial is more suitable. Check out what the job involves.' Language teachers spend a lot of their time looking for suitable published materials, adapting them and also making their own teaching materials from authentic sources and many teachers think that they could easily move into materials writing themselves. It is actually a very difficult skill and

Debbie, who has written materials herself, warns that, 'Not everyone can become a coursebook writer. To do that you have to be creative and also be willing to accept criticism.'

Many language teachers end up working for ELT publishers as sales representatives or editors, but it is not well paid and it is not as glamorous as many teachers imagine. Phiona says that, 'I sometimes get to my nine-to-five desk job and wonder if it's really me. A year ago I was climbing the Mexican pyramids.' She warns that, 'The pay's not much better than teaching, especially at the early stages. Most of the big publishers are in Oxford, Cambridge or London, so it will be a struggle financially to begin with.' She has found that money is, 'the biggest problem. In terms of lifestyle I was much better off in teaching.' If you have worked in ELT, though, you are probably someone who is not motivated primarily by money and the salaries in publishing do rise as you progress.

An important advantage for Phiona is that, 'It's stable, there's a recognized career path, something often lacking in teaching, and it's creative work,' and Jo says that moving into publishing, 'has been an excellent step'. If you enjoy working in a team and would like the stability of what Sarah describes as, 'seeing your life laid out in future books', then publishing could be right for you. The deadlines in publishing are much longer and you do not get what Phiona refers to as the, 'adrenaline rush of "teaching in 10 minutes"', as a big coursebook series can have a planning and development cycle of two or three years. Sarah is already planning until 2005 and says, 'It's so long term it maps out your life,' but you have the chance to be creative and to, 'bring talented people together and produce something successful'. The job means you work on projects to create something new and Debbie says that, 'It's great to see a book go from manuscript to finished product on the bookshop shelves.' You also avoid what Phiona remembers as, 'the monotony of repeating the same stuff in class again and again'. If you are jaded with ELT for whatever reason, but want to use what you have learned, then publishing can use your skills and experience in a different way.

Trialling and reading for publishers

Trialling and reading for publishers are not full-time jobs, but they combine well with teaching and can give you relevant experience to help you move into publishing. Some editors send out manuscripts to experienced teachers who are paid to write a report giving feedback on the material and to give their professional judgement on the originality and usability of the material. Some publishers are also looking for teachers to pilot new material with their students and to write up their opinions and comment on how their students reacted. If you are an English Language Teacher with no previous editorial experience, a possible route into editorial work is by doing freelance work for a publisher as a reader who comments on new manuscripts. You could establish contact with a publisher, perhaps by talking to their sales representative at book fairs or launches. This could lead to you being asked to do a reader's report or pilot material. You may be interested in doing this as something different on top of your teaching, but contact with publishers will also give you some insight into how they work and help you decide if this is something you would enjoy.

Sales representative

If you get a job with an ELT publisher, you may start your new career in sales. Jo started as a sales representative for one of the big publishers and says, 'It's a foot in the door as there is a lot of room for movement in the company. If you want to take a step out of ELT then publishing is an obvious avenue. Starting as a sales rep is a great way in and gives you a very good grounding for editorial work.' The job involves promoting your publisher's list to bookshops and at Trade Fairs and perhaps setting up bookstands at ELT conferences. Jo says that, 'One of the fun parts is attending conferences such as IATEFL where we have to organize stands and display materials.' You may also go into colleges and language schools, many of which have their own bookshops, to do a presentation on your publisher's list or to promote a new coursebook or dictionary. You may also arrange promotional tours and visits for authors. Jo enjoys this because, 'You have the opportunity to meet the big names of the ELT world, which can be great fun.'

Your ELT experience is useful and important as it means you know what teachers are looking for. Jo taught in Poland and Brazil before moving into publishing and says, 'I was used to being on the teacher's side of the desk looking at the books and it's still a bit strange being on the other side.' You will have had first-hand experience of some of the problems they face so you can talk about your materials with confidence and credibility as you will have probably used some of them yourself in the classroom. She says that, 'The most important thing is to have had teaching experience and to be able to relate, listen and understand what teachers and the market are saying to you. There's nothing more irritating than having someone patronize you with sales banter.' Because your job involves talking to teachers and listening to what they want from materials and what works well, you can feed back to your publisher and suggest additions to their list. Jo says the sales representative is, 'a really important link to the market. I enjoy finding out what people want and what is working well and I pass this information back to our commissioning editors.'

As a sales representative, you usually receive a basic salary, but work mainly to commission, so the harder you work the more you earn (which is certainly not the case in teaching). Before she started in publishing, Jo says, 'I wasn't really sure what a sales rep did exactly and I didn't like the idea of becoming one of those hard hitting "buy buy buy" kind of people.' In fact, the job is not like that at all and she found that, 'I don't actually sell. I listen and chat and meet some great contacts.' Jo says, 'You have to be versatile. Sometimes the day starts at five in the morning in Oxford and ends with a book display in Hastings. You need to be willing to travel and not look at your clock until the day is done.' The job involves travelling and meeting people, and Jo likes the fact that, 'It's very flexible and I can organize my own time.'

Travelling can certainly be fun, but can be quite lonely if you have to stay somewhere overnight and are on your own in a strange place in the evening. Jo is now the UK representative for one of the large ELT publishers. She gets a company car, which is a perk as, 'I've never had a car before,' but says that the sales season is quite short, so, 'We work flat out during this time. This means being away from the office and home four days a week and this can become a bit tiring.'

Some sales jobs involve travelling or living abroad, so you may be able to move into publishing if you have experience of a particular country. If you are tired of teaching, but still enjoy living and working abroad, Debbie suggests that, 'There is the possibility of working in an overseas branch of a large publishing company where you co-ordinate with schools and teachers and also advise the company about that particular market.' If you have worked abroad in one country for a while and know the market and speak the language, then working in sales could be a career shift that will use your skills and experience to advantage.

Editing

The large ELT publishers are looking to take on people with ELT experience and will train you on the job, but publishing is very popular as a career move, so there will be stiff competition for any job advertised. Sarah, who now works for one of the large ELT publishers, had two interviews and was initially turned down. She says, 'I felt devastated and very rejected, but six months later they rang up and said, 'We really liked you. Can you come for a third interview.' She was offered the job and now works as a Senior Editor, but says, 'You have to be persistent and be prepared to wait to get what you want.' Phiona, who has only recently moved into publishing, says the same thing. 'One key thing is to keep at it. Plenty of people I work with got in on their third or fourth attempt.'

Assistant editor

If a publisher takes you on, you will probably start as an assistant editor and be given training while you work. Phiona says, 'My spelling's better than it ever was as a teacher,' although there is much more involved than just proofreading. You will certainly learn about proofing symbols, but your job will be to see an author's manuscript through from commission to publication. You will work closely with designers to make sure the text fits the page, which gives you the opportunity to come up with creative ideas for problem solving, 'We have eight pages to fill, what can you think of?' Debbie says that you also, 'need to be organized and able to multitask as there are so many stages to the process and things you have to remember to meet your deadlines'. Phiona says her job as assistant editor involves three things, 'Development work, which is research, thinking about new projects and so on; content editing, which is shaping what goes into a book; and copy editing. That's the fine-toothcomb stuff: commas, hyphens and the like. You need the ability to juggle between the big picture stuff and the fiddly details like hyphens.'

Freelance editor

You may get a job in publishing and, after you have gained some experience, and built up your skills and contacts, decide that it would suit you to work freelance. Debbie worked for a couple of large publishing companies, which taught her a lot, and she now works freelance, which means, 'I get to do a bigger variety of projects.' She finds that, 'Working freelance is flexible and I am able to combine it with bringing up a family as I work from home.' Debbie now combines freelance editing with some materials writing of her own and this can work well. Working from home may suit you if you have other commitments or if you want to work part-time and combine editing with other things. It also means you do not have to live in one of the big, expensive cities where most of the big publishing houses are. Once you are known and established as a freelance editor and have built up good contacts, you can do a lot of work by phone, post and electronically by e-mail. The authors or publishers can send you the material, which you edit and return to them, so you may never actually meet them and all your work is done from home.

Senior editor

You may eventually work your way up to become a commissioning editor, which involves talking to teachers about what they want and recognizing gaps in the market. Sarah enjoys this aspect of the work and says, 'I adore developing books and courses and I love selling my ideas and presenting them. When a big project comes off, it's very satisfying to think that I planned this and found someone to write it and saw it through.' You may be sent unsolicited material and your job is to recognize potential authors and commission books for your list. You may also have regular authors with whom you work, but in both cases, you work closely with your author to ensure that they meet deadlines and that the work fits your requirements. You may also set up trials for course-books and may visit schools and colleges abroad if the book or series is targeted at a particular overseas market. The job changes as you progress, of course, and Sarah says, 'There's an increasing amount of pressure as you move up and developing books is only about a tenth of my job now.'

Lexicography

Another possibility is to move into lexicography, which is dictionary writing. Debbie, who worked as a lexicographer for one of
the big publishers when she left ELT, says, 'I learned a lot about
language and about editing. Intellectually, lexicography can be
fascinating.' Many people contribute to the writing of a dictionary
and Debbie found that, 'Working in a large team is good discipline
in terms of learning the skills.' You usually work on a discrete
section of a particular project, which may last years as, 'A major
dictionary can take up to five years to revise.' There is a very
competitive market for ELT dictionaries and working as a lexicographer may suit you if you teach part-time or have young children
and want to work from home. It can also suit you if you take
early retirement from ELT, but still want to use your skills and
experience. Most lexicographers work freelance on specific projects
and, if you are shortlisted but have no experience of dictionary
writing, the publisher will give you a test to check your lexical
aptitude. Publishers vary, of course, in the ways they recruit, but it
is unlikely that you could move straight into lexicography as soon
as you have qualified. Generally, you would need at least an ELT
diploma and varied teaching experience, so this is not a career move
you can make after the first few years.

Applying for jobs in publishing

If you are serious about wanting to move into ELT publishing, then
you need to think about how to present your skills and experience
to the best advantage. As Senior Editor, Sarah is now closely
involved in the recruitment and selection of new staff and has to
look through lots of letters from applicants. She says, 'It's insulting
when we get a badly written letter with mistakes all over it. You'd
be amazed at how many teachers send the most appalling applications. How can they think we'd take them on?' She says, 'We're
looking for someone who can construct a well-crafted paragraph
with accurate spelling and grammar. That's the first hurdle.' It
sounds obvious, but it is extremely important to check and re-check
your application as you will not be considered unless you demonstrate that you can pay attention to detail.

Many advertisements ask you to send your CV and a covering letter and it is important to make sure that you present yourself well. Again, Sarah is surprised at how poorly many teachers do this and says, 'We want something short, but informative enough to show us what someone's done and what responsibilities they've had. We don't want to have to guess how old they are or work out what went on, it needs to be clear and we don't want anything too wacky.' There are suggestions about the written aspect of job applications in Chapter 7, but is a good general rule to try and keep your CV to no more than two pages and to do the same in your letter of application because, as Sarah says, 'We haven't got time to plough through reams of stuff and we want something where the information we need is right there.'

If you are lucky enough to get offered an interview, then think carefully about the aspects of your ELT experience that are relevant to the job. Any employer is looking for a well-balanced person who will fit in with the organization, but the ability to work as part of a team is particularly important in publishing as authors, artists, editors and printers work together on the production of a book. In teaching, you often work on your own for much of the time and make your own decisions about what to teach and how to present your material, so think of occasions when you have worked collaboratively with other people and be prepared to talk about them. Explain how the team worked and give concrete examples of your contribution and what this achieved.

You also need to be able to talk about a range of ELT materials you have used. It is no good talking about, 'that grammar book with the red cover', as Sarah says that publishers are looking for people with, 'a solid knowledge of textbooks who can justify why they use them and talk about their strengths and weaknesses. We want people to show they have the ability to analyse material and who can move from the global to the particular and draw conclusions.' Do some preparation before the interview and not only check the title, publisher and author of materials you have used, but be clear about what you like or do not like about them. There is no need to be sycophantic, but it is probably a good idea to be able to talk about materials published by the people who are interviewing you and to explain why you like the books and would like to work for the organization.

Translating

You need to be a native speaker of another language or to have near-nativelike proficiency in another language to move into translation. You may have studied a foreign language for your first degree or be a non-native English Language Teacher, but using your skills in both languages could supplement your income from teaching or be a career shift for you. The work will suit you if you are patient, methodical and enjoy paying attention to detail, but you also have to have a good ear for both the languages you are dealing with as good translation usually captures the spirit of the original text. If you are translating contracts or other documents using complicated legal language however, it is vital that you are precise and accurate as a mistake could cost the company millions of pounds.

There are two main kinds of translation – work on literary texts and technical translations. There are more opportunities in technical work and it will help if you have some specialist expertise, but an understanding of the finer points of both languages is the most important thing. Pam worked at a Centre for Interdisciplinary Research at a university in Germany and this provided an opportunity to do very varied work. 'I got lots of practice in translating manuscripts in fields such as sociology, history and psychology and some of the professors I met there still send me their texts to translate.' Some places may ask for specific qualifications to prove your translation skills, but if you are living abroad and speak the language fluently, you will probably be able to pick up work.

If you are teaching for an international company or a business that wants to expand its markets, then you may also be able to use your contacts to get translation work. Pam often gets work through her teaching of Business English. 'Firms I teach at give me prospectuses, leaflets about the products they manufacture, translation of minutes of meetings, contracts and so on.' You may be happy to do this to supplement your income from teaching or you may want to give up teaching and become a translator. You are providing a specialist service and it is important not to undersell yourself. Pam says, 'I was very bad at the beginning at asking a high enough fee and letting myself be persuaded to work at lower rates.' Most translators work freelance, which can be quite insecure and lonely, but the advantage is that you can work from home and take on as much or little work as suits your situation. Working as a freelance translator could suit you if you are able to work on your own without close supervision and if you are, 'prepared to learn about different fields of work'.

Dyslexia support

If you live and work in Britain, you could use some of your language teaching skills to work providing support for people with dyslexia. This is a growing area of learning support and is provided one-to-one for adults in further education colleges or in adult education. Jackie, who now does 10 hours a week support in a large college, says that students are either referred to her through their tutors or can self-refer if they know they have a problem. For some learners the problem is very severe and they cannot read or write, but others have less severe problems and need strategies to help them with spelling. Most of the students she deals with are native speakers, but she is able to use her ELT experience as, 'In dyslexia work we use very similar activities to ESOL. We do lots of multi-sensory stuff and things like language experience and using colour.'

Jackie did a part-time 12-week course, which qualifies her to work with adults. As with any part-time course, it was hard work on top of a full teaching timetable and she had to work individually with a learner who needed support with reading and writing. The course looked at a lot of theory about how the brain works and at reasons why people are dyslexic and she had to do a diagnostic report and a case study of the learner she was working with. Jackie found it fascinating and says, 'Some people will have visual processing problems and others will have auditory processing problems, so they need different things.' Jackie had felt she was becoming rather stale in her ELT work and finds dyslexia support enables her to, 'use my imagination and creativity. You're thinking, "What new activity can I do with this person to help them?" and it's very exciting when something works.'

As a contrast to teaching large classes of ESOL learners who may only stay for a term, Jackie enjoys working with one student over a much longer timescale. 'It's rewarding to work with someone all the time they're at college. I'll see them one year and then I'll see them the next year as well, so I get to know the students and what they need.' One-to-one can be very hard work and, 'The student can take a lot out of you, which can be very draining,' but Jackie says that, 'It's very much a joint effort and you work together. You suggest strategies that they then go away and try, so it's very much a two-way process.' If you would like to introduce some variety into your pattern of work or even to move from ELT into a different sort of teaching, then dyslexia support can use some of your existing expertise and give you the opportunity to, 'see someone really develop'. There are good courses available and dyslexia support is a growing area in further education, so this is a good time to develop an additional expertise.

IT training

Moving from ELT into IT training is another possible career option if you are looking to do something different. If you have worked in a well-equipped centre either in Britain or abroad you have probably used CALL (Computer Assisted Language Learning) software with your students and you may have had to teach them the basics of how to log on and off and some very simple word-processing skills. You may also have highly developed IT skills and be familiar with a number of software packages from other areas of your life, so it may be a small step to move into training.

If you have been on IT courses yourself, you will know that the standard of training is often dreadful and that trainers rarely use the methods and activities that we take for granted in ELT as a way of actively involving the learners. Keith, who worked as an IT trainer for three years after teaching in Sri Lanka, says, 'The average EFL teacher is a lot more engaging and engaged with a group of students than the average IT trainer. They tend to do demonstrations and lectures, but EFL teachers do lots of group and pair work and get the learners doing things straight away.' The skills that you have developed in ELT are easily transferable to IT and lead to highly effective training.

Not only ex-EFL teachers think this. Cathy works for an IT training company in London, which was recently named 'Company of the Year' by the Institute of IT Training, the professional body that regulates training. She interviews prospective trainers and found that she had to, 'interview many to get a few'. All candidates who got an interview, had to deliver a 15-minute training session and those who were boring and did not involve the trainees did not get through to the next stage of the selection process. About a year ago, she noticed that out of the last couple of batches of applicants, the ones she had taken on all had an ELT qualification. She saw that there was a connection between this and being an effective IT trainer as those with an ELT background involved the trainees at once, asked questions and got trainees working together and discovering things for themselves, which is standard practice in ELT and good training practice in general. Her company now advertises for candidates with an ELT background to be IT trainers and over half of those she has recruited have been language teachers. She says they are not looking for IT expertise as they can train people up and they, 'hire for attitude and train for skills'.

If you enjoy teaching, but are tired of ELT or went into it as a way of funding your travels and now want to use your skills in a different field, then IT training could be for you. George did an ELT certificate as a way of funding his travels in Thailand and Indonesia, but says, 'It was never a career move for me and I knew that when I came back I'd need to do something different.' He says that 'IT training uses the same methods and principles as ELT, so it's an easy transition. I love it.' He also enjoys the fact that IT training is much better paid than ELT and that the work is available all year round and is not seasonal. His company does training for public and private organizations and there is no shortage of work as they can hardly keep up with the demand. George says that he still gets the rewards and pleasure of teaching and, 'the buzz of training people and knowing they've achieved something', but he also has a secure full-time job and a better salary than he would get teaching ELT in Britain.

ELT recruitment

Moving into ELT recruitment from teaching sounds a little bit like gamekeeper turned poacher, but there are lots of advantages and it is a way of using the experience you have gained by teaching and working in different countries to recruit others. If you have taught abroad, ELT recruitment can use your knowledge of the country, culture and language to help find teachers who will fit in there. Annette recruits for Italy and says, 'Because I'm an ex-teacher and because I've worked in the country I'm recruiting for, I know what they're looking for. It's about having a cultural affinity with the people you're dealing with and knowing how to deal with them, how to talk to them and how their system works.' You will recruit for the private sector, as the state sector tends to interview and appoint its own staff, and will interview EFL teachers for language schools all over the world.

Recruitment is a way of remaining involved with language teaching in a less direct way. Colin works in London for a large international company and says, 'It was always my intention to work abroad for a couple of years and then come back to the UK and settle down. This job seemed a good opportunity to develop new skills, but still in the sphere of ELT,' and Annette says, 'I'm still in ELT, but not on the teaching side.' You will still have plenty of contact with teachers and Annette values this aspect of her new career. 'ELT people are interesting. In the staffroom at lunchtime the stories exchanged are all, "When I was in China", or, "When I was in Budapest", compared to the stories that might be exchanged when bank workers or whoever are having their lunch.'

You may want to stay within the world of ELT, but be tired of the classroom yourself. Paul is now in recruitment after working in Japan and Spain and loves it partly because, 'It's not teaching. I really enjoyed my experience of it, but I wouldn't want to do it forever.' Annette was also glad to leave teaching and says, 'I loved it for all those years, but I got to the point where I thought, 'If I have to teach the present perfect one more time, I'll go mad.' Many teachers like the job, but do experience a kind of burnout. Alan, whose job in recruitment includes training, says, 'I love teaching, but you can have too much of a good thing if you're in a routine of five hours a day, five days a week.'

ELT recruitment is very big business. You will earn more than in teaching and Annette gets what she calls, 'an acceptable salary for London'. Sharon, who had been a Director of Studies before moving into recruitment, agrees that, 'It's better paid and has more possibilities than teaching.' Money was a factor in Paul's decision to move into recruitment. 'Teaching long term wasn't for me. The students were great and I had a fantastic social life, but the pay was abysmal. I came back specifically to find a job in another field.' You could:

- work for a large organization and recruit teachers for the company's own schools all over the world;

- use your expertise to recruit teachers for any school anywhere that needs staff;

- recruit teachers to work anywhere in the world;

- specialize in recruiting for a particular country that you know well.

Annette's company does all those things and she says, 'We recruit for our own schools and as an agency for other schools. If they want a teacher, we'll find one.'

If you recruit for your company's schools, your experience of teaching for them means you have the advantage of knowing how the organization works and what it is looking for. Sharon worked abroad for one of the large chains and had been a Director of Studies and so already had experience of recruiting and selecting staff. She now works in London sending teachers to her organization's schools all over the world. She does not have personal experience of all the countries she sends people to, but she does have knowledge of the organization and how it operates. All the interviews are face to face, but she also organizes large recruitment fairs all over Britain and talks to people who just turn up and are interested in the idea of ELT. At the moment, she is very busy trying to meet the demand for teachers in China and, although she misses the variety of ELT, she says, 'I wouldn't want to be a full-time teacher again.'

You do not need a recruitment background as it is your ELT experience that is relevant to the job. You need to be able to find the applicant to match the requirements of an employer and choose the right person to fit the job so that both parties are happy. This can be very satisfying and Annette travels to Italy a couple of times a year to see her clients. She says, 'It's about building up relationships with clients over the years and I meet them and they're like old friends.' She also sees the people she has recruited, which can be, 'really rewarding if you've placed someone as a teacher and you see them over there and they're having a really nice time'.

Part of your job in recruitment involves making sure teachers know what to expect in the new job and Paul says that, 'We don't want to sell jobs because people will be disappointed when they go out.' Colin finds it very satisfying when he is able to match someone to a job he knows they will enjoy and, from his own experience of working in Japan and the Czech Republic, he knows that working abroad can change your outlook on things. He likes, 'the chance to change people's lives. I had a great time abroad and I'd like to think that I can prepare people enough that they'll benefit from the opportunity.' His company organizes induction for teachers recruited for overseas and is careful to try to prepare them to live and work in a different culture. It is an important part of Colin's job satisfaction to get feedback from teachers he has placed. 'You get e-mails from teachers you've sent out to China or Taiwan and they say, "Great! Thanks. Fantastic. Thanks for preparing us so well. You're right. It does change your outlook on things".'

The world of recruitment in general has a reputation for being very high-pressured with a high staff turnover, but ELT recruitment is different and Annette says that, 'People tend to stay in recruitment as it's a really nice job.' Paul, who has just been promoted in recruitment, says, 'When you say you work in recruitment, everyone has images of really hard sell and commission, but it's really not like that in EFL recruitment.' The salary scale is also different than in commercial recruitment agencies as staff are paid a salary and do not get large bonuses or commission on each teacher appointed. The pay is still better than teaching, though, and another advantage is that, 'The office is very relaxed as there's no terrible pressure to hit targets. It's a nice working environment.'

If you would like to move into ELT recruitment, Colin says that networking is vital so it helps if you teach for a large company with schools all over the world. A lot of jobs are offered internally, so, 'It's about raising awareness of your name and abilities.' He advises that you should, 'Always maintain a high profile within the school you're in, so everybody knows your name and involve yourself in marketing activities. It doesn't matter that you're not going to get paid for it, as you'll get to know people.' If you do not work for a large international chain, then you need to make contact with and send your CV to all the major ELT recruiters. Colin suggests you should, 'Give them an update every six months of what you're up to and what you've learned and just keep pushing people to see if there are any opportunities.' If you are determined and persistent, then you will hear of vacancies when they do arise and your name will be known when you apply, which gives you an edge.

9 Top tips for a successful career

Getting your first ELT job is just the beginning of what should be a rewarding, successful career. This book includes advice from ELT teachers who work in Britain and all over the world in a variety of different settings. They include:

- teachers with MAs and people with no ELT qualifications;
- new teachers and those who have been teaching for 25 years;
- teacher trainers and recent trainees;
- part-time teachers and Directors of Studies and Heads of ELT Departments;
- teachers of adults and of young learners;
- teachers in the state and private sectors;
- teachers of ESOL and EFL.

The range and variety of teaching opportunities is enormous and there continues to be a worldwide demand for ELT. As you begin your new career, here are some top tips from other teachers, not only about how to survive, but how to enjoy ELT wherever you work.

Your first job

- Don't take the fist job that's offered unless you think it's right for you. (Sean)
- You'll need support, so find out about the organization you'll be working for and make sure you're with one that will look after you. (Neil)

▍ You've got to want to do it. It's not just for the money. (Cristine)

▍ Choose somewhere where they'll be supportive of you and won't just leave you to get on with it without finding out how you're getting on. (Patrick)

▍ It's not always a good idea to choose a job with the most well-known organization. Choose a smaller school, as long as it's a good school, and you can move up the ladder much quicker as there isn't so much competition. (Alan)

▍ Don't undersell yourself. (Pam)

▍ Go for a job with variety where you can teach different levels. (Patrick)

▍ Start gradually and don't be too ambitious in terms of the number of hours you do if that's possible. (Rachel)

▍ You need to be prepared to work a lot more than the hours in the classroom. You always work much more than you're paid for and you must be prepared for that. (Alex)

▍ The worst thing about teaching is doing too much of it. Don't take on more than you can manage. (Rodney)

▍ Show some willingness and enthusiasm about your job. It goes a long way. (Alan)

▍ Don't be so busy taking on work and planning your lessons that you just tire yourself out and don't enjoy it any more. (Andrea)

▍ Be organized. Just because teaching's usually quite informal and can be quite fun, it doesn't mean it's not a proper job. Be professional. (Andrew)

Planning lessons

▍ Be well prepared and always prepare for more than the time available, so you don't have to worry that you'll run out of material. (Sophia)

▍ To do your students justice, you have to do the preparation and know what your objectives are. (Simon)

▌ Prepare your material well and think carefully about the lesson from the point of view of the teacher and from the point of view of the learners. What are they going to get out of it and what are they going to be able to do? (Melanie)

▌ Put a little bit of your own personality in the lesson, so you don't appear like a computer presenting things. (Sophia)

▌ You have to be well prepared and to think about the dynamics of the lesson. (Melanie)

▌ Keep your lesson plans. If you do a nice lesson plan and it works well, store it away as you can use it again, which will save an awful lot of time. (Annette)

▌ Don't worry. Just make sure that when you teach, you know why you're doing things. Everything else will fall into place if you have a reason for doing everything you do. (Nathan)

▌ There are some great lessons on the Internet, so use anything you can find that works. Don't feel you've got to re-invent the wheel. (Roger)

Teaching

▌ Make sure you enjoy the lessons as the students won't if you don't. (Sean)

▌ Teaching is largely about becoming confident in the role of teacher and in what you're doing. (Paul)

▌ Learning is a matter of listening and a good teacher has the space to be able to listen to their students rather than listening to their own thoughts. (James)

▌ Don't go too fast. Teachers tend to prepare a lot of material and think they've got to get through it all and they rush through stuff and the students haven't taken any of it in. (Miranda)

▌ Learn the students' names as soon as you can. (Sean)

▌ You have to be adaptable. If something's not working it has to be changed there and then. (Melanie)

▌ Don't get carried away with lots of resources and activities and doing things with the students and forget about developing a rapport and just making a relationship with them. (Simon)

▌ It's vital to inject your own interests into the work. Whatever you're interested in and whatever your students are interested in, bring that into the teaching as that makes it come alive. (Madeleine)

▌ Be very well prepared before you go in, but also be prepared to deviate from what you've prepared and don't worry if that happens. (Miranda)

▌ Be prepared, but in class be conscious of the people you're dealing with, not your plan. (Steve)

▌ Think clearly and organize yourself beforehand, so you're not nervous and can react to what's going on in the classroom. (Aiden)

▌ Enjoy it and don't be frightened of the teaching. (Michael)

▌ You're teaching people first and the subject second. (Andrea)

▌ Don't try to be too controlling. (Andrew)

▌ Be as relaxed as possible and don't feel constrained by what you've planned. (Josephine)

▌ Don't be discouraged when things go haywire. The important thing is learning from them going haywire. (Sue)

▌ Prepare yourself professionally and then you'll be able, without dire consequences, to inject something of yourself into the lesson and you'll have the confidence to allow your personality to come through. (Gary)

▌ Don't worry if things go wrong. You'll be cringing, but the students probably won't even notice as they don't know what you've planned. (Stella)

▌ Teach the students in front of you. There's no such thing as a problem class. You've got to teach them, otherwise you're in the wrong job. (Sue)

▌ Make sure people treat you and other students with respect. (Andrew)

▌ Listen to what the students are saying and don't rush through things. (Aiden)

▌ Make sure that the students have opportunities for active learning. (Simon)

▌ Don't be too controlling. When you're nervous there's a tendency to try and dominate a class, but let the students do most of the talking. (Andrew)

▌ When you come out of the classroom thinking, 'That was alright,' that's probably the time for you to retire. (Sue)

▌ Find your own style as you can't always do what they taught you on your certificate course. (Neena)

▌ Don't be afraid to be a 'clown' at times and, most of all, don't take yourself or the English language too seriously. (Adrian)

▌ Prepare well so you know where you're going, but be prepared to feel the atmosphere. Always have something else you can do if what you've planned isn't going well. (Cristine)

▌ Listen to the students and get to know them as individuals. Show them that you're interested in them. (Neena)

▌ You've got to enjoy it. If you don't enjoy it, there's no point really. (Rachel)

Teaching resources

▌ Don't worry about being too imaginative at the beginning, but focus on the resources you've got. If you've got a coursebook, just follow that and do what the Teacher's Book says. (Patrick)

▌ Use the coursebook even if it's not ideal. So what? You haven't got all the hours in the day to re-write it. (Roger)

▌ Steal mercilessly from your colleagues and use their ideas and materials. (Jo)

▌ In order to save your life in the classroom, get a few resources. There are loads of wonderful resources around, so spend a few pounds and get some good books and cassettes and some games and flashcards. (Ricky)

It's great to follow a book at the beginning as it's a great support. You can add your own complementary ideas later when you know more. (Josephine)

The students

Always bear in mind that not all the students will approach things in the way you do. (Josephine)

If you don't know the answer to a question, tell the students that you don't know. Don't make something up as then they'll lose confidence in you as a teacher. (Annette)

Be relaxed and talk to your students as they need the chance to talk to English people. (Sean)

You need to keep the students in mind and realize that they have a personal life and that their whole life is not just coming along to you for a few hours a week. (Andrea)

Put yourself in their shoes and think about what it's like to learn a language from scratch. It's very difficult. (Josephine)

Remember you're dealing with people who have a different frame of reference to you, so try to understand what they're trying to express and how they're feeling. (Ricky)

You've got to like people. You're working with them, not just teaching them. (Andrea)

Learn something about the students' culture, something like food or music, and a bit of their language as this will help you make an emotional connection at once and break down barriers. (Aiden)

You have to bear the students in mind all the time and be aware that they're trying to cope with so many things at once. (Liz)

Learning a language is quite a personal thing and people can get embarrassed quite easily, so put yourself in their situation. (Rachel)

Getting support

▌ Don't be afraid to ask people for help. (Sean)

▌ Try to learn from other teachers and see what they're doing and observe and listen. (James)

▌ Join NATECLA, because ESOL teachers can get very isolated and you've got to know what's going on in other institutions and you need to keep on training. (Sue)

▌ Ask for help and support and don't think your questions are silly. (Miranda)

▌ Don't be too sure of yourself. If you have a very high opinion of your own teaching skills you can become inflexible, so always be open to advice. (Andrew)

▌ Ask other teachers for ideas. (Patrick)

Learning from experience

▌ It will get easier. You'll make mistakes, but be prepared to laugh about them. (Steve)

▌ You need to learn to be a little brave. If you do an activity the first time round and it doesn't really work, at least you can learn why it didn't work so you're not scared to adapt it next time. (Andrea)

▌ There's no need to be nervous, because you have what the students want, which is to be fluent in English and your job is to help them get that. (Liz)

▌ You can't ever stand still as a teacher because you'll lose the *joie de vivre* and you'll just be going through the motions. You've got to keep trying to do something different. (Andrew)

▌ You've got to be constantly willing to learn as a teacher. (Ricky)

▌ Get as much classroom experience as you can get anywhere you can get it because the more experience you can get in the classroom, the more relaxed you are. (Aiden)

▋ Just take everything you can to get as much experience as you can. If someone rings at 8.30 am and says, 'Can you cover at 9.30 am? Just say yes and you can panic on the way there. (Stella)

▋ Get a mentor if you can. (Ricky)

▋ No matter how much training you have, it's the practice that counts. (Neena)

▋ You need to keep learning as a teacher otherwise you stop dead. (Andrea)

▋ Although an ELT certificate is invaluable, it doesn't turn you into an experienced teacher. It just opens your eyes to what a good language teacher could be. (Andrea)

Working abroad

▋ Try to learn the language to help you integrate. (Sean)

▋ Get out and throw yourself into it so there's no escape. (Alex)

▋ If you're going abroad for the first time, perhaps don't go somewhere like Thailand or Indonesia that's miles away from home. Go somewhere that's easy to get home from if you need to. (Andrew)

▋ Go to interesting places and don't get bogged down. Have a good time and make the most of it. (Ricky)

▋ Working abroad is not going on holiday, so thoroughly research the place you're going to. Can you see yourself living and working in that culture? (John)

▋ Do your utmost to become involved in the culture and meet as many local people as you can. (Paul)

▋ Throw yourself into it. If you speak a bit of the language, speak to everyone in that language. (Annette)

▋ Take as much as you can with you like photos and any real British memorabilia or souvenirs as your students may never have seen a British person or been to this country. (Alex)

▌ Don't go for the ex-pat lifestyle, although it's very tempting. If you're only there for a year, you won't get much out of it. (Annette)

▌ Remain focused on the job and stick to the contract, but get out there and see different things and meet local people. (Colin)

▌ Doors will be open to you that you'd never get through at home because you're different and foreign and seen as exotic and knowledgeable and you have to use that. (Paul)

If you have read this book, you should have a good idea of whether ELT is right for you and the qualifications you need to make it a career and not just a job. If you have read this far, you may be ready to launch yourself into an area of work that is new to you and to take up the challenge of ELT. Whether you do it for a couple of years while you travel or whether you have found a career for life, you should use the advice from experienced teachers to get the most out of ELT and to enjoy working with your students in Britain or abroad.

Glossary

authentic materials   Real-life written or spoken texts that teachers use to teach English. They are not specially written for language teaching, but are examples of everyday English, which can be used in the classroom.

bilingual   Describes someone who has grown up speaking two languages at home and is comfortable speaking either.

CELTA   Certificate in English Language Teaching to Adults. This is one of the most widely recognized ELT qualifications and is accredited by UCLES.

DELTA   Diploma in English Language Teaching to Adults. This is also offered by UCLES and is an internationally recognized and respected training course.

DOS   Director of Studies. The senior person in private language schools who organizes the classes and supervises and supports staff.

EAL   English as an Additional Language. This term is used mostly in the schools sector to describe the language taught to children whose home language or mother tongue is not English.

EAP   English for Academic Purposes. This is English at an advanced level for students planning to study or studying mainstream subjects like economics or engineering at English speaking universities.

EFL   English as a Foreign Language. This describes the teaching of English to people who are learning the language for pleasure, work or educational reasons.

ELT English Language Teaching to non-native speakers of the language. It is an umbrella term, but does not cover teaching English to native speakers in schools and colleges.

ESOL English for Speakers of Other Languages. This is the English taught to people who have settled in Britain, but speak a different first language or mother tongue.

ESP English for Special or Specific Purposes. This is English that people need for specialist purposes like medicine, technology or tourism.

mother tongue The first language a person learns to speak at home with her/his mother.

native speaker Someone who grows up speaking English at home.

TEFL and **TESOL** Teaching English as a Foreign Language and Teaching English to Speakers of Other Languages.

UCLES University of Cambridge Local Examinations Syndicate. This is the examination and awarding body that has developed some of the main teacher training courses for ELT. It also administers the main internationally recognized exams for EFL.

VSO Voluntary Service Overseas. The body that organizes voluntary placements for teachers from Britain in developing countries.

Further information

Recommended reading

It is not worth buying lots of books until you are sure you would like to work in ELT, but here are some useful resources, which are worth looking at to help you get a flavour of ELT, and to use once you start teaching.

English teaching methodology
Harmer, J (2000) *How to Teach English*, Pearson
This is extremely useful for trainees taking a CELTA course or any other new, inexperienced teacher. It is clearly written and has good advice about teaching methods and ideas for lesson planning. It is a very good, practical guide to the why and how of ELT.

Scrivener, J (1994) *Learning Teaching*, Macmillan/Heinemann
This is an excellent introduction to the theory and practice of ELT and is very widely recommended on ELT training courses. It is clearly written, has lots of good advice and includes very practical suggestions about what to do in the classroom. It is user-friendly and includes tasks to try out and commentaries that you can compare with your own answers.

English grammar
Collins COBUILD English Grammar, HarperCollins
This reference grammar is useful for teachers and advanced students of English. It is clearly laid out and concentrates on the real patterns of language use in everyday English. The explanations are straight-forward and there is an accompanying book of exercises with practice material for you to check your own understanding.

Parrott, M (2000) *Grammar for Language Teachers*, CUP
This is particularly useful for trainee teachers as it helps develop an overall knowledge and understanding of English grammar and provides a quick source of reference in planning lessons and helping learners with problem areas. It includes useful consolidation exercises, which give you the chance to test the rules against real language use and to evaluate classroom and reference materials.

Materials for the General English classroom
Hadfield, J *Communication Games*, Longman
Incorporating *Beginner's Communication Games*, *Elementary Intermediate and Advanced Communication Games*.
This series of games and activities is photocopiable and there is a book at each level from beginner to advanced. It gives the teacher detailed advice about how to set up each activity and includes indexes of the language practised in each game. The books are invaluable for both experienced and inexperienced teachers.

Hadfield, J and C (2000) *Oxford Basics*, OUP
This is a series of short, very accessible books, which introduce teachers to ways of helping learners communicate in the classroom. They give ideas and clear guidance and are for lower-level classes. Titles include: *Presenting New Language, Classroom Activities, Simple Listening Activities, Simple Rewarding Activities, Simple Writing Activities, Simple Speaking Activities.*

Watcyn-Jones, P *Penguin Photocopiable Resource Books*, Pearson
Incorporating *Pair-Work 1 (Elementary to Pre-Intermediate)* and *Pair-Work 2 (Intermediate to Upper-Intermediate)*.
This series gives teachers lots of good classroom materials and ideas to use in the classroom. Students are given the chance to practise communication skills in a natural, fun way. Students work in pairs and each student is given different information on the same subject so they have to talk to each other to complete the activity successfully.

Keeping in touch
EL Gazette
This is a monthly global ELT newspaper, which includes international ELT news, teaching tips, instant lessons as well as articles on management issues. The focus is really EFL and does not include

ESOL, but it is a useful way to keep up to date in the field of ELT generally as it includes book reviews and interviews with key figures and writers. It comes with *EL Prospects*, which advertises ELT jobs worldwide.

English Language Teaching Guide (10th edn, *EL Gazette*)
This is issued yearly and is a very useful guide to teaching EFL in the private sector and is recommend by the British Council. It has pages of listings covering initial and advanced ELT qualification courses and a country by country guide with recruitment information and schools listings. It includes lists of useful addresses of schools all over the world and gives advice about getting into ELT as well as progressing.

Language Issues (NATECLA)
This journal is published twice a year and includes articles, book reviews, reports and research papers. It looks at issues in ESOL, community language training, anti-racism and Language Support and Development in Britain.

Materials for young learners
Phillips, S *Young Learners*, OUP
This gives teachers advice and ideas for teaching English to children from 6 to 12 and has lots of activities for the classroom including arts and crafts, games, stories, poems, puppets and songs. It also includes photocopiable worksheets and is a good resource for new as well as more experienced teachers.

Reilly, V and Ward, S *Very Young Learners*, OUP
This book has more than 80 ideas for teaching children aged three to six and includes games, songs, drama and art as well as practical advice. It also has photocopiable worksheets and flashcards, which you can use in class.

Working abroad
Griffith, S (2000) *Teaching English Abroad*, Vacation Work
If you know you want to work abroad then this book is extremely useful as it includes advice about training courses in Britain and overseas. It also has a detailed country by country guide with lots of information about how to get work, red tape, conditions of employment and prospects for qualified and unqualified teachers. It is written in a very user-friendly style and is regularly updated.

Useful Web addresses

There is now a huge virtual world of ELT as many organizations and institutions have their own Web pages and there are a number of interactive bulletin boards, which allow you to talk to other teachers. Many pages include links to other useful sites, but the suggestions below are sites that include teaching ideas and materials to get you started as well as coordinating and training bodies.

BASELT (The British Association of State Colleges in English Language Teaching)
BASELT is the body that coordinates state organizations in Britain that offer accredited ELT courses and that employ qualified teachers. Organizations apply for BASELT approval and there is a free annual booklet, which lists all member organizations. If you want to work in the state sector, it is worth checking to see if your potential employers are listed.
e-mail: baselt@chelt.ac.uk
http://www.baselt.org.uk

BATQI (British Association of TESOL Qualifying Institutions)
This is a voluntary association of UK colleges, schools and universities that run courses that lead to recognized ELT qualifications. It has a code of practice for organizations and publishes a register of BATQI accredited courses. If you want to do an ELT course, it is worth checking to see if it is accredited.
e-mail: g.m.clibbon@bristol.ac.uk
http://www.batqi.org

The British Council
The British Council recruits teachers to work at its overseas language centres. For most jobs it is looking for people with a diploma-level qualification or a PGCE in TEFL and two years' experience, but some countries will take you with certificate-level qualifications if you have some experience. It is particularly interested if you also have experience in special areas like young learners or Business English. It advertises for specific jobs in the *Times Educational Supplement* and *The Guardian* and lists current vacancies on its Web site.
e-mail: teacher.vacancies@britishcouncil.org
http://www.britishcouncil.org/english/engvacs.htm

EF (English First)
EF is one of the largest chains of private language schools world-wide and recruits qualified teachers for positions in Britain and abroad. If you do not have a qualification, EF offers its own, free one-month TEFL certificate with automatic placement on successful completion of the course.
e-mail: recruitment.uk@englishfirst.com
http://englishfirst.com

English-to-Go
This is a site to browse through if you are looking for ready-made lessons on a specific topic or at a particular level. All the lessons are based on authentic, current news stories and come with sug-gested activities and detailed teachers' notes. It is particularly useful if you are starting out and need some ideas, you are very busy and need something to fill a gap or if you have students with an interest in a particular topic, eg 'health and medicine' and you are looking for material. Once you register, you receive weekly tips, a grammar and a 'warmer' activity as well as a 'free lesson'.
http://www.english-to-go.com

GAP Activity Projects
GAP Activity Projects organizes a variety of projects for students who want to do something challenging in the year between school and university. You can apply to work in ELT in one of the devel-oping countries and, if accepted, you attend a one-week teacher training course.
http://www.gap.org.uk

International House
International House specializes in teaching EFL and in teacher training courses in ELT. There are over 90 schools in 20 countries affiliated to the central organization in London and it recruits trained teachers with UCLES (or equivalent) certificate and diploma qualifications to teach in its schools. It also runs training for ELT managers.
e-mail: info@ihlondon.co.uk
http://www.ihworld.com

NATECLA (National Association for Teaching English and Other Community Languages to Adults)
NATECLA is the professional organization for ESOL and Community Language teachers. It is organized into local branches, which run training sessions to meet local and national needs. It also campaigns on a variety of educational issues connected with the needs of asylum seekers and refugees. It holds an annual conference and publishes a newsletter with articles, reports, reviews and teachers' tips. It also publishes a journal exploring current issues in ESOL.
e-mail: co-ordinator@natecla.fsnet.co.uk
http://www.natecla.org.uk

Saxoncourt and English Worldwide
Saxoncourt and English Worldwide is the biggest commercial recruiter of EFL teachers in Britain and it recruits for clients all over the world as well as its own schools. At the moment, it is particularly looking for teachers in the Far East and Eastern Europe. It advertises a list of vacancies on its Web site.
e-mail: recruit@saxoncourt.com
http://www.saxoncourt.com

Saxoncourt Teacher Training
Saxoncourt Teacher Training is a non-profit-making part of the organization that provides pre- and in-service teacher training in ELT. At present, it is the only centre in Britain to offer the UCLES Certificate course for teaching young learners.
e-mail: christopher@shane-english.co.uk
http://www.saxoncourt.com

Tower of English
This site has a wide variety of ELT resources and is good for teaching ideas and online exercises.
http://members.tripod.com/~towerofenglish

Trinity College London
Trinity College London offers well-recognized ELT certificate- and diploma-level courses in Britain and overseas and these are accepted by employers in the UK and worldwide. Courses are offered only by validated and approved centres and all include a teaching

practice component as well as written assignments. You can get a list of centres in Britain and abroad that offer Trinity qualifications.
e-mail: info@trinitycollge.co.uk
http://www.trinitycollege.co.uk

UCLES (University of Cambridge Local Examinations Syndicate)
UCLES offers the two best-known ELT qualifications, which are recognized and valued by employers in Britain and worldwide. There are very rigorous quality controls of training centres and trainers and courses are carefully monitored to maintain high standards. Courses include supervised teaching practice as well as written assignments. UCLES will be able to give you information on centres in Britain and abroad offering its courses.
e-mail: efl@ucles.org.uk
http://www.cambridge-efl.org.uk

UCL grammar site
This is designed for students of English and is clear and easy to use. It is useful for trainee certificate- or diploma-level teachers as well as a refresher for practising teachers.
http://www.ucl.ac.uk/internet-grammar/

VSO (Voluntary Service Overseas)
VSO recruits newly qualified and experienced teachers of ELT for placements in 36 countries overseas. The ELT placements are usually for two years and are very varied. They include secondary school classroom teaching as well as teacher training and provide a very good opportunity to use your existing skills to help developing countries while learning lots of new skills and gaining valuable experience.
e-mail: enquiry@vso.org.uk
http://www.vso.org.uk

Index

adult education 16–22
  home tutors *see* volunteers
  students 17–18
  working conditions 19

BATQUI (British Association of
  TESOL Qualifying
  Institutions) 120
Business English 37–38, 62–64

Certificate in English Language
  Teaching to Adults (CELTA)
  see qualifications
Certificate in English Language
  Teaching to Young Learners
  (CELTYL) *see* qualifications
certificate courses (CELTA and
  Trinity) 99–107
  assessment 104, 112
  costs 104–05, 112
  course content 102–04, 111–12
  entry requirements 101–02,
    108–11
  ESOL specific *see* qualifications
  intensive courses 105–06
  part-time 106–07
  Post Graduate Certificate of
    Education (PGCE) *see*
    qualifications
  trainees 100–01
  Young Learners Extension
    Certificate *see* qualifications

DELTA *see* diploma qualifications
diploma qualifications (DELTA
  and Trinity) 112–18

assessment 115
  costs 116
  course content 114–15
  distance learning 117–18
  entry requirements 113–14
  intensive courses 116
  part-time 116–17
distance learning 98, 117–18, 124

EAP 13
EFL 12, 25, 36–37
  students 18, 25, 36–37
ESP 13
ESOL 12, 17–18, 24–25, 96–97
  qualifications *see main entry*
  students 17–18, 24–25
  volunteer training 96–97

finding a job 126–41
  application 131–33, 133–35
  cold calling 130
  general advice 131–33
  interview preparation 133–36
  interviews 136–39
  newspapers 126–27
  phone interviews 139–40
  recruitment agencies 127
  turning up abroad 128–30
  using contacts 128
first job 76–79, 143–47, 164–71
  contract 77–79
  getting support 170
  getting the most from the job
    145–47
  icebreakers 142–43

learning from experience
170–71
lesson planning   143–44,
165–66
materials   144–45,   168–69
paperwork   76–77
preparation   141–42
students   169
teaching   166–68
further education   23–30
language support   25–26
social programme   27
students 24–25
summer schools   27–28
training   28
working conditions   28–30

in-company teaching   62–64

job hunting _see_ finding a job

language support _see_ further
education

masters degrees   121–25
assessment   125
costs   125
course content   124–25
entry requirements   122
distance learning   124
full-time   123
part-time   123

private language schools   35–45,
64–69
Business English   37–38
one-to-one   66–67
social programme   38–39, 69
summer schools   43–45
students 36–37
training   39–40
working conditions   41–43,
67–68
private training providers   30–31
students   30

working conditions   31
private tutoring   45–48, 59–62
boundaries   61–62
children   51–52
factors   61
home teaching   46–48
in-company   62–63
publishing   149–56
applying for jobs   155–56
editing   153–54
lexicography   155
sales representative   151–53
trialling and reading   150–51

qualifications   93–107, 108–25
CELTA   99–107
CELTYL   109–12
Certificate in Teaching ESOL
97
ELT management courses   121
ESOL specific   95–98
introductory courses   94–95
masters degrees _see main entry_
Postgraduate Certificate of
Education   118–20
Trinity Certificate   99–107
Trinity Diploma   113–18
Young Learners Extension
Certificate   109–12
qualities _see_ skills and qualities

related careers   148–63
dyslexia support   158–59
ELT recruitment   160–63
IT training   159–60
publishing   _see main entry_
translating   157–58

skills and qualities   1–6
personality   4
qualities   3
skills   5
summer schools   43–45
children's summer schools
48–51

residential summer
  schools 44–45

teaching 7–10, 45–48, 59–62,
  165–68
  abroad *see* teaching abroad
  best things 7–9
  home teaching 46–48
  private tutoring 45–46,
    59–62
  top tips 165–71
  worst things 9–10
teaching abroad 53–55, 75–90
  accommodation 79–81
  contract 77–79
  learning the language 81–85
  making friends 85–90
  paperwork 76–77
teaching children *see* young
  learners
Trinity Certificate *see*
  qualifications

universities 32–34, 74
  abroad 74
  foundation courses 32
    on-course support 33
    pre-sessional courses
      32–33

volunteers 20–22, 55–59, 96
  classroom volunteers 21–22
  community organizations 22
  gap year 55–57
  home tutors 20–21
  summer courses 57–58
  training 96
  Voluntary Service Overseas
    (VSO) 58–59

working abroad 75–90, 171–72
  accommodation 79–81
  contract 77–79
  friends 85–90
  learning language 81–85
  VSO *see* volunteers

young learners 14, 15, 23, 48–52,
  69–74, 109–12
  CELTYL 109–12
  private lessons 51–52, 70
  private sector 14, 70–73
  qualifications 109–12
  state sector 15
  schools 15, 23, 73–74
  Saturday schools 51
  summer schools 48–51
  Young Learners Extension
    Certificate 109–12

Index of Advertisers

European University viii, 91
Leeds Metropolitan University Centre for Language Study 92
School of Linguistics and Applied Studies v
University of Cambridge LES vi
University of Leeds ii